# DIABETES
# COOKBOOK

# *Delish*

# DIABETES COOKBOOK

70 delicious and healthy recipes for every meal

HEARST BOOKS
New York

# Contents

# foreword

"What can I eat?" is usually the first question that a person asks when they learn they have diabetes. As a diabetes educator for over 20 years, I am always happy to inform people with diabetes that the days of "allowed foods" and "forbidden foods" are long gone. Indeed, research has shown that the very same diet recommended for the rest of the population—one that includes plenty of fresh fruits and vegetables, whole grains, low-fat dairy products, lean meats, fish, poultry, legumes, and, yes, even an occasional piece of cake, dish of ice cream, or some other sweet treat—is the best diet for people with diabetes. In other words, the person with diabetes does not have to purchase "diet" food or cook special meals.

*Delish Diabetes Cookbook* is a simple yet comprehensive answer to the question, "What can I eat?" It will allow you to effortlessly translate the dietary recommendations into adventurous, flavorful, and "delish" recipes— recipes that will undoubtedly defy what you may expect from a cookbook for people with diabetes. These 70 recipes take you around the world—from India (mango lassi) to Thailand (chicken and vegetable rice paper rolls) to Mexico (spinach and cheese quesadillas) to the United Kingdom (fish and oven-roasted chips) to Italy (tomato, bean, and pasta soup) to China (garlic shrimp and bok choy with herbed rice) to Japan (seared tuna with chilled soba) to Australia (curried lamb pockets). There are also a generous array of more familiar recipes like berry buckwheat pancakes and chicken and bacon club sandwiches. The large variety of legume-based recipes, like pumpkin and split pea tagine, offer a tasty alternative to meat-based meals. Finally, you will be delighted by the dessert recipes, which include tiramisu, honey buttermilk ice cream, and cherry upside-down cake.

*Delish Diabetes Cookbook* can help you to look at your life with diabetes as an opportunity to try new foods, spices, and cooking methods, and a chance to improve your health as well as the health of all those you cook for. I encourage you to jump in with both feet—you'll be glad you did!

Joyce M. Vergili, EdD, RD, CDE

# about diabetes

## What is diabetes?

Diabetes is a condition in which the amount of glucose (sugar) in the blood is too high. This is because the pancreas does not make enough insulin or the insulin that it does produce is unable to do its job properly. Insulin is needed by the body to move glucose from the blood stream into the muscles and cells to be used for energy.

## Dealing with diabetes

In this book we have set out to give advice on how to eat well, enjoy healthy foods, and keep blood glucose levels managed. We encourage you to increase your physical activity. Current guidelines recommend that you engage in aerobic exercises, such as walking, for at least 30 minutes a day most days of the week (for a total of at least 150 minutes per week) and in resistance training at least two times a week. It is very important to discuss any increase or change to your exercise routine with your doctor or diabetes educator.

## There are two main types of diabetes

Type 1 diabetes is an autoimmune disease in which the body actually destroys the cells that produce insulin, so there is no insulin present. It represents 5 percent of all cases of diabetes and normally occurs in children or young adults but can also occur in adults. While we don't know the exact cause of type 1 diabetes, it is thought that some people have a genetic predisposition for this condition and, when exposed to a trigger, possibly a viral infection, the immune system then destroys the insulin-producing cells in the pancreas. Type 1 diabetes is not caused by lifestyle factors. People with type 1 diabetes require insulin injections several times a day for life.

Type 2 diabetes has various risk factors such as family history or lifestyle. It results in not enough insulin to meet the body's need or the insulin that is produced is no longer working efficiently to move glucose from your blood into your cells (known as insulin resistance). It represents 90 to 95 percent of all cases of diabetes. Lifestyle factors such as unhealthy eating and lack of physical activity can contribute to the development of type 2 diabetes. Other risk factors include family history, large waist circumference ("apple" shape), being overweight, certain ethnic backgrounds, and pre-diabetes. Pre-diabetes is a condition that occurs when the blood glucose level is higher than normal but not high enough to be diagnosed as diabetes.

Type 2 is the most common form of diabetes. While it usually affects adults, more young people, and even children, are being diagnosed all the time. Often symptoms of type 2 diabetes go unnoticed as the disease develops gradually. Symptoms may include unusual thirst, frequent urination, extreme hunger, blurred vision, frequent infections, cuts and bruises that are slow to heal, and tingling and numbness in the feet. Sometimes no symptoms are noticed at all. Persistent high blood glucose (sugar) levels in either type 1 or type 2 diabetes can damage the body's organs. This damage is referred to as diabetes-related complications.

Healthy eating along with an active lifestyle can assist in the prevention and management of type 2 diabetes. A healthier lifestyle will not only help you to maintain a healthier body weight, but it also helps manage cholesterol, blood pressure, and blood glucose levels. If you are using insulin or medication to help control blood glucose levels, you should discuss any dietary changes with your doctor, dietitian, or diabetes educator to maintain a safe balance.

# High glucose levels can affect:

**Vision** Diabetic retinopathy is the leading cause of blindness in Americans between the ages of 20 and 74. The development of retinopathy is strongly related to the length of time diabetes has been present and the degree of blood glucose control. Scheduling a dilated-pupil eye exam at least once a year and getting treatment for any damage that may occur can prevent blindness caused by retinopathy.

**Kidney function** Your kidneys help to clean your blood. They remove waste from the blood and pass it out of the body in the urine. Over time diabetes can create damage to the kidneys that causes them to leak. In fact, diabetes is the leading cause of kidney failure. There are no symptoms of kidney damage until it's quite advanced, so it is important you have your kidney function checked yearly to detect any problems. Your kidneys are also affected by high blood pressure so you should get that checked at least every three months.

**Circulation and sensation to the lower limbs** Peripheral neuropathy (nerve disease) and damage to blood vessels may lead to lack of sensation, leg ulcers, and serious foot problems from which lower limb amputation may result. Poorly controlled diabetes is the number one cause of non-traumatic lower limb amputation. Personal daily foot checks and thorough annual foot examinations conducted by your doctor or podiatrist will help to reduce your risk of lower limb complications.

**Large blood vessels** People with diabetes are at increased risk of heart disease and stroke associated with high blood glucose levels, high blood pressure, and cholesterol. High glucose levels can also increase the risk of infection, gum disease, and delay wound healing.

While these complications are serious and can be life threatening, with appropriate lifestyle changes and attention to blood glucose control, people with diabetes can substantially reduce the risk of developing these complications.

## Managing diabetes

Type 2 diabetes cannot be cured. It can, however, be managed by adopting a healthy lifestyle and taking pills and/or insulin, as prescribed by your healthcare provider. Genetics does play a part in determining a person's weight and the likelihood of developing type 2 diabetes. An unhealthy diet high in saturated fat, low in fiber (i.e., low in vegetables, fruit, and whole grain breads and cereals), high in calories (from too much fat, sugar, alcohol, and larger portion sizes), and a lifestyle low in physical activity increases the risk of developing diabetes and other health problems. Three evenly spread meals a day can prevent blood glucose levels from rising too high after eating.

While each person with diabetes has different dietary needs, general recommendations for daily intake are to eat 6 servings of grains (bread, pasta, rice, cereal, tortilla)—of which at least 3 servings should be whole grains (e.g., whole wheat bread, brown rice); 3–5 servings of vegetables, including 2 servings of dark green vegetables (e.g., spinach, broccoli) and 4 servings of red and orange vegetables (e.g., tomato, carrot, sweet potato) each week; 2–4 servings of fruit—preferably in its whole form, rather than as juice; 2–3 servings of low-fat dairy products (e.g., milk and yogurt); 5 to 6 ounces of lean meat, fish, poultry, eggs, and low-fat cheese, or other protein-rich foods such as legumes (dried beans, peas, and lentils) and tofu; and small amounts of heart-healthy (unsaturated) fats and oils (see serving sizes table, top of page 13).

## Talk to your doctor

The information in this book provides basic guidelines to healthy eating for people with diabetes. Not all recipes in this or any cookbook are necessarily appropriate for all people with diabetes, nor will all recipes fit into every meal plan. All the recipes in this book have been reviewed by a Registered Dietitian/ Certified Diabetes Educator and are consistent with the nutrition recommendations as set forth by the American Diabetes Association.

The American Diabetes Association recommends that you work with your healthcare provider, diabetes educator, or dietician to design a meal plan that is right for you and includes foods you enjoy. A key message for people with diabetes is that foods high in carbohydrates raise your blood glucose levels more than foods that are low in carbohydrates.

For many people with diabetes, eating 45-60 grams of carbohydrate at each meal is about right. Some people with diabetes will also need to eat a snack or two; snacks should generally provide about 15-30 grams of carbohydrate. The best way to know how new foods or recipes affect your blood glucose level is to check it about 1-2 hours after you eat. If your blood glucose level is above the goal range set by your healthcare team, then you may need to eat a smaller portion or talk to your dietician for alternative strategies. Desserts were included in this book to be used sparingly and should be discussed beforehand with your dietician.

Along with exercise and medications, healthy food choices are important for good diabetes management. By eating well-balanced meals with an appropriate amount of carbohydrates, you can keep your blood glucose levels within the target range.

## Healthy snacks

The aim is to make meals that are full of flavor and color and well-balanced for good health. If you enjoy a snack between meals, keep the snack small and select healthy options such as those listed below. Snacks are not required by everyone; speak to your dietitian.

| | |
|---|---|
| FRUITS | 1 small apple or orange, 1 medium peach, ½ mango, 1 kiwi, 2 small plums. Berries and melons are very low in sugar so the recommended portion sizes of these fruits are larger than for most fruits (e.g., 1/3 cantaloupe, 1¼ cups or 1 large slice watermelon, 1¼ cup strawberries, 1 cup raspberries) |
| VEGETABLES | Vegetable sticks: celery, carrot, snow peas, peppers |
| NUTS | 1 ounce unsalted nuts (e.g., 14 walnut halves, 20 almonds, 35 peanuts, 50 pistachios) |
| BREADS | 1 slice (1 ounce) raisin or multigrain toast |
| CEREAL | ½ cup high-fiber breakfast cereal with ½ cup 1% low-fat milk |
| DRINKS | 1 cup skim café latte or small hot cocoa |
| CAKES | Small (1¼ -inch square) unfrosted brownie or small Danish or 1-inch slice banana nut bread or small cupcake |
| SAVORY | 2 rice cakes or 3 high-fiber crispbread crackers topped with cottage cheese, slice of tomato and chives, or half an English muffin with 1 slice reduced-fat cheese and slice of tomato, or 2 pita triangles |
| DAIRY | ½ cup sugar-free pudding or ½ cup eggnog or 6-ounce container of low-fat yogurt |

Vitamin D deficiency has recently been associated with the development of type 2 diabetes. The main source of vitamin D comes from exposure to sunlight. Foods containing vitamin D include oily fish (salmon, mackerel, sardines, and herring), eggs, and fortified foods (such as margarine). It is unusual for people to obtain adequate levels of vitamin D through dietary sources alone. Your doctor can order a simple blood test to assess your vitamin D level. If you are deficient, your doctor may recommend that you take vitamin D supplements.

| FOOD GROUP | 1 serving is equal to |
|---|---|
| GRAINS, BREADS, CEREALS | 1 slice (1 ounce) of bread or ⅓ cup of cooked pasta or rice (= 1 ounce uncooked pasta or rice) or ½ cup of cooked cereal (e.g., oatmeal) or ½ cup starchy vegetable (e.g., potato, sweet potato, corn) or 1 tortilla (6 inch diameter) or 1 pancake (4 inch diameter) or 1 ounce (about ¾ cup) ready-to-eat cereal |
| VEGETABLES | 1 cup raw vegetables or ½ cup cooked vegetables or ½ cup 100% vegetable juice |
| FRUIT | 1 small or ½ large piece of fruit (e.g., 1 small apple, ½ banana) or ½ cup 100% fruit juice or ¼ cup dried fruit |
| DAIRY | 1 cup fat-free or 1% milk or 1 cup fortified soy milk or 1 cup fat-free or low-fat yogurt |
| PROTEIN | 1 ounce lean meat, poultry, seafood, or 1 egg or 1 ounce low-fat cheese or ½ cup (4 ounces) tofu or ½ cup cooked beans, peas, or lentils |

## Carbohydrates

Carbohydrate-rich foods are the best source of energy for the body. When carbohydrate foods are digested they break down into glucose. By eating regular meals and evenly spreading your intake of carbohydrate foods throughout the day, you will maintain your energy levels without causing large spikes in your blood glucose levels. The American Diabetes Association recommends 45 to 60 grams of carbohydrate at each meal as a reasonable place to start, but you may need more or less than that. A Registered Dietitian or a Certified Diabetes Educator can develop an individualized meal plan for you that matches the foods you like to eat to your body's carbohydrate requirements. When choosing carbohydrate-rich foods, choose those that are higher in fiber and lower in fat, such as whole grain bread, brown rice, and fresh fruit and vegetables. These foods are more nourishing and have a lower glycemic index, which means they have a smaller impact on your blood glucose level. Because all people need energy, approximately half of your calories should come from carbohydrates.

## Managing your lifestyle

Keep a record of your food intake, physical activity, and blood glucose levels. This allows you to determine the impact of food, physical activity, and your diabetes medicine (pills and insulin) on your blood glucose levels (BGLs).

If you find that your BGLs are elevated 2 hours after a meal:

1. You may have eaten more carbohydrates than usual at your meal. If so, reduce the amount eaten next time and measure your BGL to determine the impact.

2. Consider swapping high GI carbohydrate foods for lower GI options (see the section on Low GI Foods, page 17).

3. Go for a walk.

4. Talk to your dietitian and diabetes team; if your blood glucose elevation is not lifestyle related, you need to discuss your diabetes treatment with your healthcare team.

Note: elevated BGLs can be due to other causes including illness or infection.

## Carbohydrate foods include:

- Bread—choose whole grain bread; check for the word "whole" on the ingredient list (i.e., "whole wheat", not just "wheat") and make sure each slice contains at least 2 grams of fiber
- Cereals—choose high-fiber varieties such as rolled oats, bran cereals, and granola
- Pasta, rice, and other grains such as barley, bulgur, and couscous—choose whole wheat pasta and brown rice
- Starchy vegetables—potatoes, sweet potato, yams, and sweet corn
- Legumes—beans, peas, and lentils (e.g., baked beans, kidney beans, chick peas, and split peas) are high in both protein and in carbohydrate; therefore, they are a tasty alternative to meat, fish, and poultry, as well as to potato, pasta, and rice
- Fruit—all fruits, including apples, oranges, peaches, bananas, berries, and melons, are a good source of fiber (but fruit juice is not!)
- Milk, milk substitutes, and yogurt—choose low-fat (1%) or fat-free varieties of milk, soy milk, (calcium-fortified) and yogurt
- Desserts—Less nutritious forms of carbohydrate include chocolate, cakes, cookies, pastries, candy, regular ice cream, and soft drinks. Because these foods are high in fat and sugar, it's best to eat them only occasionally.

## Fat

Fats have the highest calorie content of all the nutrients. Eating too much fat may result in excess weight, which in the long run makes it more difficult to manage your blood glucose levels. A healthy eating plan, which is lower in fat, particularly saturated fat, is advised to help prevent and manage type 2 diabetes.

### Saturated fat

It is important to limit saturated fat because it raises total and LDL (bad) cholesterol levels. Saturated fat is also linked with insulin resistance. Saturated fat is found in animal foods such as fatty meat, full-fat dairy products, butter, and cheese. It is also found in palm oil (found in solid cooking fats, snack foods, or convenience foods) and coconut products such as shortening, coconut oil, and coconut milk.

### Not all fats are unhealthy

Some fat is important for good health. Mono and polyunsaturated fats do not raise cholesterol levels. Use a variety of monounsaturated and polyunsaturated fats to achieve a good balance. These include:

• **Monounsaturated fats**—sources include most nuts, avocados, and olive oil.

• **Polyunsaturated fats**—sources include walnuts and oily fish, which contain omega-3, and seeds and seed oils, for example sesame and safflower, which contain omega-6.

Almonds, cashews, hazelnuts, macadamias, peanuts, pecans, and pistachios are higher in monounsaturated fats while Brazil nuts, pine nuts, and walnuts have more polyunsaturated fats. Walnuts are one of the few plant foods that contain the essential omega-3 fat, alpha-linolenic acid (ALA), with smaller amounts also found in pecans, hazelnuts, and macadamias.

Instead of frying, try steaming, roasting, or grilling foods. You will be pleasantly surprised at how good steamed foods taste.

## What is Glycemic Index (GI)?

Glycemic Index (GI) is a measure of a food's impact on blood glucose levels. Foods with a low GI (GI less than or equal to 55) are digested more slowly than foods with a high GI, and slower digestion means slower absorption of glucose into the bloodstream. In other words, your blood glucose levels will not increase as quickly when eating low GI foods, such

## Non-Starchy Vegetables

Vegetables are divided into two groups—starchy and non-starchy. The starchy vegetables include potatoes, sweet potatoes, and corn, and each ½ cup serving contains about the same amount of carbohydrate (15 grams) and calories (80) as a piece of bread. The non-starchy vegetables contain very little carbohydrate—only about 5 grams, and very few calories—only about 25, per ½ cup serving. This means they have little impact on your blood glucose levels or your weight. Feel free to fill up on these diabetes-friendly powerhouses:

• Artichoke
• Asparagus
• Beans (green, wax, Italian)
• Bean sprouts
• Beets
• Bok choy
• Broccoli
• Brussels sprouts
• Cabbage
• Carrots
• Cauliflower
• Celery
• Cucumber
• Eggplant
• Kale
• Leeks
• Lettuce
• Mushrooms—all kinds
• Onions
• Peppers (all varieties)
• Radishes
• Salad greens
• Spinach
• Summer squash
• Sugar snap peas
• Tomato—fresh or canned
• Zucchini

## Shopping advice

• **Never shop for food when you are hungry.**

• **Make a shopping list and stick to it. This prevents the temptation to add chips and candy to the cart.**

• **Shop when you have plenty of time, so you can read the nutritional information on packages and won't be tempted to make bad choices because you're in a hurry.**

• **Stick to the perimeter of the supermarket. This is where you find the fresh fruit, veggies, meat, and dairy.**

• **As American author and food activist Michael Pollan advises: Don't buy anything your great-grandmother wouldn't recognize as food. This eliminates most over-processed foods.**

as a boiled sweet potato, compared to eating higher GI foods, such as a boiled white potato. There are many factors that determine a food's GI. The higher the fiber content, the lower the GI. That's why an orange has a lower GI than orange juice—the fruit has 10 times more fiber than the juice! Another factor is the way the food is cooked. For example, pasta has a higher GI when overcooked than when cooked al dente.

According to the American Diabetes Association, it is more important to consider the total amount of carbohydrate consumed rather than the type of carbohydrate (i.e., low or high GI). However, choosing low GI foods may provide some additional benefit to blood glucose control as well as to overall health—foods that have high GI tend to be less nourishing (e.g., white rice) than their lower GI counterparts (i.e., brown rice).

## Low GI pantry staples

High quality whole grain bread—whole or cracked grains; in baked goods, use oat bran, rice bran, or rolled oats instead of flour if suitable for the recipe.

Rice—basmati and long-grain brown rice rather than jasmine or short-grain rice, or use pearl barley, bulgur, buckwheat, or couscous.

Orange-fleshed sweet potato or yam in preference to most varieties of white potato. Sweet potato is higher in fiber, which helps to slow the digestion and absorption of glucose into the blood. It is also lower in starch than most varieties of white potato and therefore has a lower GI value. Most varieties of white potatoes have a high GI because they contain large amounts of easily digested starches that produce a rapid rise in blood glucose levels. Some varieties of new potatoes have lower levels because they have higher levels of harder-to-digest starch, but most are still considered moderate-to-high.

## Eating out

This is one situation where you have minimal control on the size of the portion on your plate, and to a lesser extent, how the food is cooked. However, you can select each dish wisely.

- Pick the whole wheat roll.
- No butter.
- For an entrée, choose a salad-based dish, steamed vegetables, or soup instead of anything deep-fried.
- Be aware of your total carbohydrate intake and how it is prepared. Be cautious of fries or mashed potatoes, pasta, rice, and breads prepared with butter, creamy sauces, or cheese.
- Select a salad accompaniment, roasted or steamed vegetables without a cream-based sauce or butter. Ask if the chef will add ground black pepper and fresh lemon juice as a substitute.
- Some meals provide excess food. Consider asking for a smaller portion, or whether you can order an appetizer as a main course.
- Eating Italian? Avoid the heavy lasagnas and creamy pasta sauces. Instead, select a dish with fresh tomato sauce. The same suggestions apply to dining in an Indian or classic French restaurant.
- When faced with a buffet, choose healthier foods over those you know aren't good for you. Try to keep in mind the limits of the carbohydrates for each serving.
- When dining at a friend's or relative's house, tell them beforehand that you are following a carbohydrate-conscious low-fat diet. You may want to offer to bring a side dish or dessert.
- Desserts can be oh-so tempting. Fresh fruit and yogurt are good choices. A good restaurant will ask the chef to make it fresh for you.
- Alcohol: If you drink alcohol, do so in moderation. "Moderate" means no more than two drinks per day for men and no more than one drink per day for women. One drink is 12 ounces beer, 5 ounces wine, 1½ ounces distilled spirit. Consume alcohol only when eating a meal—never on an empty stomach.

## Low GI foods

- Fruit—apples, apricots, bananas, grapefruit, grapes, kiwifruit, oranges, peach, pears, plums
- Al dente pasta
- Legumes
- Sweet corn
- Peas
- Add lentils, split peas, barley, and dried beans to soups and casseroles.
- Add lentils, canned beans, and even rolled oats to rice dishes in combination with the meat base.
- Breakfast cereals—use unprocessed rolled oats, oat bran, rice bran, or lower-fat granola.
- Jam—look for 100 percent fruit varieties and use without butter.
- Milk should be low-fat or non-fat.
- Pasta—all varieties are low GI, but whole grain varieties are a better choice because they have a higher fiber, vitamin, and mineral content.
- Vinegar and vinaigrette dressings can lower blood glucose levels by slowing the rate of food emptying from the stomach. Red or white wine vinegars are both good choices.
- Yogurt is best bought in the low-fat variety. No-added-sugar versions are better choices.

## Portion control

Never pile food higher than a deck of cards.
Diameter of inside rim of plate is 8 inches.
Plate is divided to match these groups.

Lean protein
3 ounces chicken
breast or fish
filet or
lean steak

Vegetables/salad
(eat as much as you like)

Lettuce, leafy salad
mixes, broccoli,
broccolini,
asparagus,
celery,
green beans,
beets, tomatoes,
cabbage,
peppers,
cauliflower,
cucumber,
mushrooms, onion,
leeks, spinach,
yellow (summer) squash,
brussels sprouts,
zucchini, radish

High-fiber/low GI carbohydrate

Couscous, pasta, or brown rice,
or whole grain bread, or sweet
potato or corn on the cob

## Before going out

You can apply a few strategies to avoid overeating when you dine out. One is
to drink a full glass of water before leaving home; another is to eat a small
snack such as a small cup of soup or a small plate of leafy green salad so that
you are not that hungry when it is time to order.

There is a lot of diet information available from your doctor and your
dietitian as well as from the America Diabetes Association. Read all you can
and make a plan that will help you deal with diabetes without changing your
life too much.

## Visual reminder using your hand—per serving

**three middle fingers together**
- size of potato

**palm of hand**
- portion of cooked fish, skinless chicken, or lean meat

**length of thumb**
- amount of low-fat salad dressing
- amount of avocado

**fist**
- approximately 1 cup fresh fruit; 1 serving of low-fat milk or yogurt

**tip of thumb**
- amount of unsaturated oil; amount of jam/peanut butter
- amount of soft (tub) margarine

**center of cupped palm (approximately 1½ ounce serving)**
- amount of unsalted nuts or reduced-fat cheese

## About the recipes

We provide the calorie content so you can stay within the recommended calorie intake guidelines. Daily calorie intake requirements vary among individuals according to your age, body weight, level of physical activity, and whether you need to lose or gain weight.

### Calories
The average adult daily calorie requirement is around 1500–2000 calories.

### Total fat
Daily intake should be limited to 20-35 percent of total calories; that is, about 40–65g of fat per day.

### Saturated fat
Saturated fat intake should be less than 7 percent of total daily calorie requirement; that is, no more than 10–15g daily.

### Carbohydrates
Daily intake should be 50–60 percent of total calories; that is, 200–250g per day. Use low GI, high-fiber carbohydrate sources where possible.

### Dietary fiber
Recommendations are 14g of fiber for every 1000 calories consumed, or about 21-28g of dietary fiber daily.

### Protein
Protein intake should be 10–15 percent of total daily calories. As a guideline, allow 0.4g of protein for each pound of your ideal body weight; e.g., a person whose ideal body weight is 150 lbs requires about 60g of protein a day.

# 7 day menu planner

| DAY | BREAKFAST | SNACK | LUNCH |
|---|---|---|---|
| MONDAY | Oatmeal with banana and walnuts (page 30) plus 1 slice whole grain bread | ¼ cup unsalted nuts | Cheese and salad sandwich (page 57) plus a green salad |
| TUESDAY | Blueberry muffin (page 38) plus 1 small container low-fat fruit yogurt | 1¼ cup strawberries | Butternut squash soup (page 57) plus a green salad |
| WEDNESDAY | Rolled barley fruit trifle (page 35) plus 1 slice toasted whole wheat bread with soft (tub) margarine | 1 banana | Chickpea salad (page 53) |
| THURSDAY | Cheesy corn on rye (page 41) | 1 small container low-fat fruit yogurt | Tuna, celery, and dill sandwich (page 51) plus a green salad |
| FRIDAY | Bran and cranberry muesli (page 42) | ½ cup blueberries plus 1 small container low-fat fruit yogurt | Chicken and vegetable rice paper rolls (page 54) |
| SATURDAY | Oven-baked rösti with breakfast beans (page 36) | 1 small container low-fat fruit yogurt | Asparagus frittata with arugula (page 69) |
| SUNDAY | Breakfast berry smoothie (page 27) | 1¼ cup strawberries plus 1 small container low-fat fruit yogurt | Carrot and lentil soup with caraway toast (page 70) plus a green salad |

This menu planner is a guide only. Eat a balanced diet to get all your required nutrients.

| SNACK | DINNER | DESSERT |
|---|---|---|
| 1 apple plus 1 small container low-fat fruit yogurt | Fish and oven-roasted chips (page 129) plus a green salad | Cranberry macerated berries (page 137) |
| 1 pear | Thai basil chicken stir-fry (page 90) | Mango, berry, and passion-fruit frozen yogurt (page 140) |
| 1 small container low-fat fruit yogurt | Seared tuna with chilled soba (page 117) plus a green salad | Tiramisu (page 149) |
| 2 kiwifruit | Chili coriander lamb and barley salad (page 84) | Citrus salad (page 138) |
| 1 orange | Steaks with pepper salsa (page 94) plus steamed beans and a green salad | Rosewater and raspberry gelatin (page 144) |
| 1¼ cup straw-berries | Herb stuffed chicken with tomato salad (page 83) | Vanilla ice cream with mango and berry coulis (page 143) |
| ¼ cup unsalted nuts | Linguine marinara (page 85) plus a green salad | Baked apples with berries (page 145) plus 1 small container low-fat fruit yogurt |

See page 11 for daily recommended intakes.

# breakfast

# smoked salmon and poached eggs on rye

serves 4

4 large eggs
6–8 large spears (6 ounces) asparagus, halved crosswise
4 slices (4 ounces) rye bread, toasted
6 ounces smoked salmon
2 tablespoons fresh chervil leaves

1 Half fill a large shallow frying pan with water; bring to a boil. Break one egg into cup, slide into pan. Repeat with remaining eggs; when all eggs are in pan, allow water to return to a boil.

2 Cover pan, turn off heat; stand about 4 minutes or until a light film sets over egg yolks. Remove eggs, one at a time, using slotted spoon; place spoon on paper-towel-lined saucer briefly to blot up poaching liquid.

3 Meanwhile, boil, steam, or microwave asparagus until tender; drain.

4 Divide toast among serving plates; top each with salmon, asparagus, then egg. Serve garnished with chervil.

prep + cook time 15 minutes
nutritional information per serving
211 calories; 16.2g carbohydrate; 1.9g fiber; 7.6g fat (2.0g saturated fat); 196mg cholesterol; 575mg sodium; 18.0g protein; low GI

# mango lassi

serves 2

1 medium ripe mango (15 ounces), peeled, coarsely chopped
1 cup 1% buttermilk
⅓ cup low-fat fruit-flavored yogurt
2 tablespoons lime juice

**1** Blend ingredients until smooth. Pour into glasses; serve immediately.

prep time 10 minutes
nutritional information per serving 198 calories; 38.9g carbohydrate; 2.6g fiber; 2.3g fat (1.2g saturated fat); 10mg cholesterol; 161mg sodium; 7.5g protein; low GI

# breakfast berry smoothie

serves 1

½ cup (3 ounces) frozen mixed
   berries
½ cup chilled 1% low-fat milk
¼ cup (2½ ounces) low-fat vanilla-
   flavored yogurt
1 shredded wheat cereal biscuit
   (½ ounce), crushed

**1** Blend ingredients until smooth.
Pour into glass; serve immediately.

prep time 5 minutes
nutritional information per serving
217 calories; 42.0g carbohydrate;
5.0g fiber; 2.8g fat (1.2g saturated
fat); 11mg cholesterol; 105mg
sodium; 10.5g protein; low GI

# blueberry hotcakes

1 large egg, separated
2 egg whites, extra
½ cup apple sauce
1 teaspoon vanilla extract
3 cups (24 ounces) low-fat yogurt
1¾ cups whole wheat self-rising
    flour
1½ cups fresh blueberries

**1** Beat all egg whites in small bowl with electric mixer until soft peaks form.

**2** Combine egg yolk, apple sauce, extract, 2 cups of the yogurt, flour, and half the blueberries in large bowl; fold in egg whites, in two batches.

**3** Spray a small skillet with cooking spray and heat over medium; pour ¼ cup batter into pan. Cook until bubbles appear on surface. Turn hotcake; cook until browned lightly. Remove from pan; cover to keep warm. Repeat with remaining batter.

**4** Serve hotcakes with remaining yogurt and blueberries.

prep + cook time 35 minutes
nutritional information per serving
260 calories; 46.9g carbohydrate; 4.7g fiber; 2.7g fat (1.4g saturated fat); 38mg cholesterol; 593mg sodium; 13.2g protein; low GI

tip Blueberries, with their juicy center and sweet taste, have become one of our all-time favorite berries.

# oatmeal with banana and walnuts

serves 4

2 cups water

1 cup 1% low-fat milk

1⅓ cups rolled oats

2 medium bananas (14 ounces), thickly sliced

½ cup (2 ounces) walnuts, coarsely chopped

1 tablespoon honey

1⅓ cups 1% low-fat milk, extra

**1** Combine the water and milk in medium saucepan; bring to a boil. Reduce heat; add oats. Simmer, stirring, about 5 minutes or until oatmeal is thick and creamy.

**2** Serve oatmeal topped with banana, nuts, honey, and extra milk.

prep + cook time 15 minutes
nutritional information per serving
329 calories; 44.8g carbohydrate; 5.3g fiber; 12.9g fat (1.8g saturated fat); 9mg cholesterol; 82mg sodium; 13.0g protein; low GI

# bircher muesli (granola) with figs and pistachios

serves 4

1½ cups rolled oats
¼ cup oat bran
¼ cup natural bran flakes
¾ cup 1% low-fat milk
¾ cup orange juice
¾ cup (7 ounces) low-fat Greek-style yogurt
½ teaspoon ground cinnamon
½ cup (2 ounces) roasted pistachios, coarsely chopped
1 large orange (11 ounces), segmented
2 medium fresh figs (4 ounces), thinly sliced

**1** Combine cereals, milk, juice, yogurt, and cinnamon in large bowl. Cover, refrigerate overnight. Stir in half the nuts.
**2** Divide muesli among serving bowls; top with orange segments, figs, and remaining nuts.

prep time 15 minutes
(+ refrigeration)
nutritional information per serving
342 calories; 52.7g carbohydrate; 7.9g fiber; 11.3g fat (2.2g saturated fat); 6mg cholesterol; 62mg sodium; 14.5g protein; low GI

# cheese and herb egg-white omelette

12 egg whites

4 scallions, thinly sliced

¼ cup finely chopped fresh chives

¼ cup finely chopped fresh chervil

½ cup finely chopped fresh flat-leaf parsley

⅓ cup (1½ ounces) coarsely grated reduced-fat cheddar cheese

⅓ cup (1 ounce) coarsely grated reduced-fat mozzarella cheese

4 slices (4 ounces) whole wheat bread, toasted

**1** Preheat broiler.

**2** Beat a quarter of the egg whites in small bowl with electric mixer until soft peaks form; fold in a quarter of the combined scallions and herbs.

**3** Spray an 8-inch skillet with cooking spray and warm it over low heat. Pour the eggs into the pan and cook, uncovered, until omelette is browned lightly underneath.

**4** Sprinkle a quarter of the combined cheeses over half the omelette. Place pan under broiler until cheese begins to melt and omelette sets; fold omelette over to completely cover cheese. Carefully slide onto serving plate; cover to keep warm.

**5** Repeat process with remaining egg white, scallion and herb mixture, and cheese to make a total of four omelettes. Serve omelettes with toast and extra chopped herbs.

prep + cook time 35 minutes
nutritional information per serving
199 calories; 18.8g carbohydrate; 2.7g fiber; 4.3g fat (1.9g saturated fat); 10mg cholesterol; 436mg sodium; 20.6g protein; low GI

# rolled barley fruit trifle

serves 4

8 ounces (about 20 medium)
  strawberries, quartered
1 medium mango (15 ounces),
  coarsely chopped
2 cups (16 ounces) low-fat yogurt
½ cup rolled barley flakes
2 tablespoons ground flaxseed
2 tablespoons ground sunflower
  seeds
1 tablespoon ground almonds
1 tablespoon honey

**1** Combine strawberries and mango in small bowl.
**2** Divide half the fruit between four 1½-cup glasses. Top with half the yogurt. Divide barley, ground flaxseeds, ground sunflower seeds, ground almonds, honey, and remaining yogurt among glasses.
**3** Cover glasses and remaining fruit separately; refrigerate overnight.
**4** Top trifles with remaining fruit to serve.

prep time 15 minutes
(+ refrigeration)
nutritional information per serving
254 calories; 41.2g carbohydrate; 53g fiber; 6.9g fat (1.6g saturated fat); 7mg cholesterol; 90mg sodium; 11.1g protein; low GI

# oven-baked rösti
# with breakfast beans

serves 4

1 medium sweet potato (8 ounces),
  coarsely grated
1 medium potato (7 ounces),
  coarsely grated
1 teaspoon coarse cooking
  (kosher) salt
1 egg
2 tablespoons whole wheat self-
  rising flour
1 small red onion (3½ ounces),
  chopped finely
2 teaspoons olive oil

BREAKFAST BEANS
2 teaspoons olive oil
1 medium yellow onion (4 ounces),
  thinly sliced
2 cloves garlic, crushed
14-ounce can diced tomatoes
¼ cup water
14-ounce can cannellini beans,
  rinsed, drained
¼ cup coarsely chopped fresh flat-
  leaf parsley

**1** Make breakfast beans.
**2** Preheat oven to 400°F.
**3** Combine sweet potato, potato, and salt in medium bowl; stand 5 minutes then squeeze out liquid.
**4** Whisk egg in medium bowl; whisk in flour. Stir in potato mixture and onion.

**5** Heat oil in large ovenproof frying pan over medium heat; add potato mixture, press down firmly. Cook rösti about 3 minutes or until browned lightly underneath. Transfer pan to oven; bake, uncovered, about 20 minutes or until browned. Turn rösti onto chopping board, cut into eight wedges; serve with breakfast beans.

BREAKFAST BEANS Heat oil in medium saucepan over medium heat, add onion and garlic; cook, stirring, until onion softens. Stir in undrained tomatoes, the water and beans; bring to a boil. Reduce heat; simmer, uncovered, about 10 minutes or until thick. Remove from heat; stir in parsley.

prep + cook time 40 minutes
nutritional information per serving
278 calories; 44.6g carbohydrate; 8.0g fiber; 6.8g fat (1.1g saturated fat); 47mg cholesterol; 616mg sodium; 9.9g protein; medium GI

tips Cannellini beans are amazingly good for you. They are loaded with nutrients including iron, magnesium, and folate, and are an excellent source of fiber.

If your frying pan handle is not ovenproof, wrap it well in aluminum foil to protect it in the oven. We used a frying pan with a base measuring 9 inches.

# blueberry muffins

makes 12

1 cup white self-rising flour

1 cup whole wheat self-rising flour

½ cup firmly packed light brown sugar

2 large egg whites, beaten lightly

⅓ cup unsweetened apple sauce

¾ cup 1% low-fat milk

4 ounces (1 cup) fresh or frozen blueberries

**1** Preheat oven to 350°F. Line 12-hole (⅓-cup) muffin pan with paper liners.

**2** Sift flours into large bowl; stir in sugar.

**3** Stir in combined egg whites, apple sauce, and milk. Do not over-mix; mixture should be lumpy. Add berries; stir through gently.

**4** Divide mixture into lined pan. Bake about 20 minutes. Cool muffins in pan 5 minutes before turning, top-side up, onto wire rack to cool.

prep + cook time 35 minutes
nutritional information per muffin
121 calories; 27.8g carbohydrate; 1.9g fiber; 0.2g fat (0.1g saturated fat); 1mg cholesterol; 287mg sodium; 3.3g protein; medium GI

tip Store muffins in an airtight container for up to two days, or freeze for up to one month.

# breakfast fry-up

serves 4

4 medium plum tomatoes
(10 ounces), quartered

2 tablespoons balsamic vinegar

7-ounce container button
mushrooms, thickly sliced

½ cup loosely packed fresh basil
leaves

¼ cup coarsely chopped fresh
flat-leaf parsley

4 large eggs

6 ounces shaved low-sodium
lean ham

8 slices whole wheat bread,
toasted

**1** Preheat oven to 400°F.

**2** Combine tomato and half the vinegar in medium shallow baking dish; spray lightly with cooking spray. Roast about 20 minutes.

**3** Meanwhile, spray a medium frying pan with cooking spray and heat over medium heat. Cook the mushrooms and vinegar until tender; stir in herbs. Transfer to serving dishes; cover to keep warm.

**4** Wipe the pan clean, spray with cooking spray, and fry eggs as desired. Remove eggs from pan. Heat ham in same pan. Serve eggs, ham, mushrooms, and tomato with toast.

prep + cook time 35 minutes
nutritional information per serving
343 calories; 38.6g carbohydrate; 4.9g fiber; 9.3g fat (2.4g saturated fat); 209mg cholesterol; 762mg sodium; 24.8g protein; low GI

# scrambled eggs florentine

serves 4

4 large eggs
6 large egg whites
2 tablespoons 1% low-fat milk
2 tablespoons finely chopped
  fresh chives
2 teaspoons olive oil
6 cups (4 ounces) baby spinach
  leaves
8 slices whole wheat bread,
  toasted

**1** Whisk eggs, egg whites, milk, and chives in medium bowl. Heat oil in large frying pan over low heat, add egg mixture; cook, stirring, until creamy.
**2** Place spinach in colander over sink; pour about 2 cups of boiling water over it. Drain well.
**3** Serve spinach and eggs with toast.

prep + cook time 20 minutes
nutritional information per serving
317 calories; 37.1g carbohydrate; 5.8g fiber; 9.3g fat (1.9g saturated fat); 186mg cholesterol; 485mg sodium; 20.9g protein; low GI

# cheesy corn on rye

serves 2

10-ounce can unsalted corn
  kernels, rinsed, drained
2 tablespoons low-fat ricotta
  cheese
2 cups (1½ ounces) baby spinach
  leaves
2 slices rye bread, toasted

**1** Heat corn in medium heatproof
bowl in microwave oven on HIGH
(100%) about 30 seconds; stir in
cheese and spinach.
**2** Serve toast topped with corn
mixture.

prep + cook time 5 minutes
nutritional information per serving
183 calories; 33.8g carbohydrate;
6.5g fiber; 2.9g fat (0.5g saturated
fat); 5mg cholesterol; 257mg
sodium; 8.6g protein; low GI

# bran and cranberry muesli (granola) serves 6

1 cup rolled oats
¾ cup all-bran
¼ cup sweetened dried
  cranberries
2 cups 1% low-fat milk
1 large banana (8 ounces), thinly
  sliced
1 cup (4 ounces) fresh raspberries

**1** Combine oats, bran, and cranberries in small bowl.
**2** Place ⅓ cup oat mixture in each bowl; top with milk, banana, and raspberries.

prep time 10 minutes
nutritional information per serving
152 calories; 31.3g carbohydrate; 4.5g fiber; 2.3g fat (0.7g saturated fat); 5mg cholesterol; 64mg sodium; 6.1g protein; low GI

tip If you don't want to use dried cranberries, use golden or dark raisins.

# berry buckwheat pancakes

1 cup whole wheat self-rising flour

½ cup buckwheat flour

1 tablespoon superfine sugar

½ teaspoon ground cinnamon

2 large eggs, beaten lightly

1⅓ cups 1% low-fat milk

1 cup frozen mixed berries, thawed

2 tablespoons orange juice

1 tablespoon confectioners' sugar

⅔ cup (6 ounces) plain low-fat yogurt

**1** Combine flours, superfine sugar, and cinnamon in medium bowl; gradually whisk in combined eggs and milk until batter is smooth. Cover, refrigerate 30 minutes.

**2** Meanwhile, blend or process berries, juice, and confectioners' sugar until pureed.

**3** Spray a medium frying pan with cooking spray and set it over medium heat. Pour ⅓ cup batter into it, and spoon 1 level teaspoon of berry puree on top of pancake batter; using skewer, gently swirl puree through batter to marble. Cook pancake until bubbles appear on surface. Turn pancake; cook until browned lightly. Remove from pan; cover to keep warm.

**4** Repeat process, using ⅓ cup batter and 1 teaspoon puree for each pancake, to make a total of eight pancakes.

**5** Serve pancakes with the remaining berry puree and yogurt.

prep + cook time 25 minutes (+ refrigeration)
nutritional information per serving 296 calories; 50.8 carbohydrate; 4.8g fiber; 4.4g fat (1.7g saturated fat); 100mg cholesterol; 521mg sodium; 14.5g protein; medium GI

tips Buckwheat flour is available in health food stores or the health food section in supermarkets.

Serve pancakes with fresh berries.

# lunches & light meals

# vegetable burgers

2 teaspoons olive oil

1 large yellow onion (6 ounces), finely chopped

7-ounce container button mushrooms, coarsely chopped

1 large red bell pepper (6 ounces), finely chopped

1 clove garlic, crushed

1 cup red lentils

1 cup low-sodium vegetable stock

1 cup water

1½ cups cooked brown long-grain rice

2 tablespoons finely chopped fresh flat-leaf parsley

⅓ cup all-purpose flour

2 medium carrots (5 ounces), coarsely grated

¾ cup (6 ounces) plain low-fat Greek-style yogurt

1 tablespoon finely chopped fresh mint

8.25-ounce can sliced beets, drained

1½ cups (2 ounces) alfalfa sprouts

2 medium tomatoes (10 ounces), thinly sliced

6 small (1.5 ounce) whole wheat rolls, split, toasted

**1** Heat oil in large frying pan over medium heat, add onion, mushrooms, peppers, garlic, and lentils; cook, stirring, until vegetables soften. Add stock and the water; bring to a boil. Reduce heat; simmer, uncovered, stirring occasionally, about 10 minutes or until lentils are tender and stock is absorbed. Remove from heat. Stir in rice, parsley, flour, and half of the carrot; cool.

**2** When cool enough to handle, shape mixture into six patties; place on parchment-paper-lined tray. Cover; refrigerate 2 hours or until firm.

**3** Spray a large frying pan with cooking spray and heat over medium heat. Cook the patties until browned on both sides and heated through.

**4** Meanwhile, combine yogurt and mint in small bowl.

**5** Sandwich patties, remaining carrot, beets, alfalfa, tomato, and yogurt mixture between toasted roll halves.

prep + cook time 1 hour (+ refrigeration)

nutritional information per serving 398 calories; 70.4g carbohydrate; 11.9g fiber; 5.7g fat (1.1g saturated fat); 2mg cholesterol; 290mg sodium; 19.1g protein; medium GI

tip You need to cook ½ cup brown long-grain rice for this recipe.

# tuna, celery, and dill sandwich    makes 2

5-ounce can chunk tuna in
 springwater, drained, flaked
2 stalks celery (5 ounces),
 trimmed, finely chopped
¼ small red onion (1 ounce),
 finely chopped
2 tablespoons low-fat ricotta
 cheese
1 tablespoon coarsely chopped
 fresh dill
2 teaspoons rinsed, drained baby
 capers
1 cup (¾ ounce) baby spinach
 leaves
4 slices rye bread, toasted

**1** Combine tuna, celery, onion, cheese, dill, and capers in medium bowl.
**2** Sandwich spinach and tuna mixture between bread slices.

prep time 10 minutes
nutritional information per sandwich
290 calories; 40.9g carbohydrate;
5.7g fiber; 3.5g fat (0.5g saturated
fat); 43mg cholesterol; 846mg
sodium; 26.9g protein; medium GI

tip If taking this sandwich to work, make the filling the night before. Put it in the refrigerator when you arrive at work. Toast the bread and assemble the sandwich at work.

# chickpea salad

serves 2

4 ounces canned unsalted chickpeas (garbanzos), rinsed, drained

1 Lebanese cucumber (4 ounces), coarsely chopped

½ small red onion (2 ounces), thinly sliced

10 pitted kalamata olives

⅓ cup coarsely chopped fresh flat-leaf parsley

½ small yellow bell pepper (3 ounces), coarsely chopped

1 small plum tomato (2 ounces), seeded, coarsely chopped

2 tablespoons low-fat tzatziki

2 slices whole wheat bread, toasted

LEMON DRESSING
¼ teaspoon finely grated lemon rind
1 tablespoon lemon juice
1 teaspoon olive oil
¼ teaspoon ground cumin

**1** Make lemon dressing.
**2** Combine chickpeas, cucumber, onion, olives, parsley, peppers, tomato, and lemon dressing in medium bowl.
**3** Serve salad topped with tzatziki; accompany with toast.

LEMON DRESSING Combine ingredients in screw-top jar; shake well.

prep time 15 minutes
nutritional information per serving
278 calories; 37.3g carbohydrate; 6.5g fiber; 10.0g fat (1.5g saturated fat); 3mg cholesterol; 524mg sodium; 10.0g protein; medium GI

tip Tzatziki is a Greek yogurt dip made with cucumber, garlic, and sometimes chopped fresh mint. It's available, ready-made, from supermarkets and delicatessens, or can be made easily at home.

# chicken and vegetable rice paper rolls

serves 6

1 quart water

2-inch piece fresh ginger (¾ ounces), thinly sliced

12 ounces chicken breast filets

4 ounces bean thread noodles

1 teaspoon sesame oil

1 tablespoon lime juice

2 tablespoons sweet chili sauce

24 x 8-inch rice paper rounds

48 large fresh mint leaves

48 fresh coriander (cilantro) sprigs

2 medium carrots (5 ounces), coarsely grated

2 medium red bell peppers (8 ounces), thinly sliced

2 medium yellow bell peppers (14 ounces), thinly sliced

4 ounces snow peas, thinly sliced

COCONUT DIPPING SAUCE

1 teaspoon sesame oil

2 cloves garlic, crushed

2 scallions, thinly sliced

2 teaspoons finely grated fresh ginger

1½ cups light coconut milk

1 teaspoon fish sauce

2 tablespoons lime juice

1 tablespoon sweet chili sauce

**1** Place the water and ginger in medium saucepan; bring to a boil. Add chicken, reduce heat; simmer gently, uncovered, about 10 minutes or until chicken is cooked through. Remove from heat; stand 10 minutes. Remove chicken with slotted spoon; discard liquid. When cool, thinly slice chicken. Cover, refrigerate 1 hour.

**2** Meanwhile, make coconut dipping sauce.

**3** Place noodles in large heatproof bowl, cover with boiling water; stand until tender, drain. Combine noodles in same bowl with oil, juice, and sauce.

**4** Dip one rice paper round into bowl of warm water until soft; place on board covered with clean tea towel. Place 2 mint leaves and 2 coriander sprigs in center of rice paper; top with a little of the carrot, peppers, snow peas, noodles, and sliced chicken. Fold and roll to enclose filling. Repeat with remaining ingredients to make a total of 24 rolls. Serve rolls with coconut dipping sauce.

COCONUT DIPPING SAUCE Heat oil in small saucepan over medium heat, add garlic, onion, and ginger; cook, stirring, until fragrant. Add coconut milk; bring to a boil. Reduce heat; simmer, uncovered, about 5 minutes or until mixture is thickened slightly. Strain mixture through fine sieve into small bowl; discard solids. Stir in fish sauce, juice, and sweet chili sauce; cool.

prep + cook time 1 hour 15 minutes (+ refrigeration)
nutritional information per serving 388 calories; 59.4g carbohydrate; 3.4g fiber; 8.2g fat (4.1g saturated fat); 36mg cholesterol; 345mg sodium; 19.3g protein; medium GI

*tip* You need one large bunch of fresh mint and another of fresh coriander for this recipe.

# butternut squash soup

serves 4

1 teaspoon olive oil

1 leek (7 ounces), thinly sliced

1 clove garlic, crushed

1 teaspoon ground cumin

½ teaspoon ground coriander

2 pounds peeled butternut squash, coarsely chopped

1 potato (11 ounces), chopped

1 cup reduced-sodium chicken stock

3 cups water

2 teaspoons fresh thyme leaves

4 slices whole wheat bread, toasted

**1** Heat oil in saucepan over medium heat; cook leek and garlic, stirring, until leek is tender. Add spices; cook, stirring, until fragrant.

**2** Add squash, potatoes, stock, and the water to pan; bring to a boil. Reduce heat; simmer, covered, about 20 minutes or until vegetables are tender. Cool 10 minutes.

**3** Blend or process mixture, in batches, until smooth. Return mixture to pan; stir until hot. Garnish soup with thyme; serve with toast.

prep + cook time 35 minutes
nutritional information per serving
258 calories; 53.6g carbohydrate; 10.3g fiber; 2.6g fat (0.2g saturated fat); 0mg cholesterol; 300mg sodium; 8.6g protein; low GI

# cheese and salad sandwich

serves 4

¾ cup (6 ounces) low-fat cottage cheese

⅓ cup (1½ ounces) coarsely grated reduced-fat cheddar cheese

½ cup finely shredded baby spinach leaves

½ cup (4 ounces ) unsalted canned corn kernels, rinsed, drained

1 scallion, thinly sliced

1 small carrot (2 ounces), finely grated

1 tablespoon sesame seeds, toasted

2 teaspoons lemon juice

½ cup (1 ounce) mesclun

8 slices whole wheat bread

**1** Combine cheeses, spinach, corn, scallion, carrots, seeds, and juice in medium bowl.

**2** Sandwich mesclun and cheese mixture between bread slices.

prep + cook time 15 minutes
nutritional information per serving
276 calories; 39.6g carbohydrate; 5.8g fiber; 5.7g fat (1.5g saturated fat); 9mg cholesterol; 517mg sodium; 16.5g protein; medium GI

# tomato, sweet potato, and brown rice salad

serves 4

1 cup (8 ounces) brown long-grain rice

1 medium orange sweet potato (8 ounces), coarsely chopped

2 cups (8 ounces) red grape tomatoes, halved

2 scallions, thinly sliced

⅓ cup firmly packed fresh small basil leaves

2½ cups (1½ ounces) trimmed arugula leaves

BALSAMIC DRESSING

2 tablespoons orange juice

1 tablespoon balsamic vinegar

1 teaspoon olive oil

1 clove garlic, crushed

**1** Cook rice in large saucepan of boiling water, uncovered, about 30 minutes or until tender; drain. Rinse under cold water; drain.

**2** Meanwhile, boil, steam, or microwave sweet potato until tender; drain.

**3** Make balsamic dressing.

**4** Combine rice, sweet potatoes, and dressing in large bowl with tomato, onion, basil, and arugula.

BALSAMIC DRESSING  Combine ingredients in screw-top jar; shake well.

prep + cook time 40 minutes
nutritional information per serving
221 calories; 43.0g carbohydrate; 3.1g fiber; 2.5g fat (0.2g saturated fat); 0mg cholesterol; 19mg sodium; 4.8g protein; medium GI

# spinach and cheese quesadillas

serves 8

⅔ cup (5 ounces) low-fat cottage cheese

4 cups (3 ounces) baby spinach leaves

1 medium avocado (8 ounces), finely chopped

1 cup (7 ounces) unsalted canned Mexican-style beans, drained

2 cups (10 ounces) unsalted canned corn kernels, drained

2 medium tomatoes (8 ounces), seeded, finely chopped

1 small red onion (3 ounces), finely chopped

2 medium zucchini (8 ounces), coarsely grated

16 x 6-inch flour tortillas

1 cup (3½ ounces) coarsely grated reduced-fat mozzarella cheese

¼ cup loosely packed fresh coriander (cilantro) leaves

**1** Blend or process cottage cheese and spinach until smooth.

**2** Combine avocado, beans, corn, tomato, onion, and zucchini in medium bowl.

**3** Preheat broiler.

**4** Place eight tortillas on baking sheets; spread spinach mixture over tortillas, leaving ¾-inch border around edge. Spread avocado mixture over spinach mixture; top each with the remaining tortillas.

**5** Sprinkle mozzarella over quesadilla stacks. Cook quesadillas under broiler until browned lightly. Serve garnished with coriander.

prep + cook time 40 minutes
nutritional information per serving 360 calories; 48.2g carbohydrate; 10.4g fiber; 13.1g fat (5.1g saturated fat); 9mg cholesterol; 724mg sodium; 16.6g protein; low GI

tips Quesadillas are filled tortillas that are broiled or fried and served with fresh salsa. They are best eaten as soon as they are cool enough to handle.

Serve with grated cabbage and carrot salad tossed in a lime juice and fresh coriander dressing.

# hummus

2 large whole wheat pita breads

1 tablespoon lemon juice

½ small yellow onion (1 ounce), finely chopped

1 clove garlic, crushed

½ teaspoon ground cumin

1¼ cups (6 ounces) canned chickpeas (garbanzos), rinsed, drained

¼ cup 1% low-fat milk

¼ teaspoon sesame oil

2 teaspoons finely chopped fresh coriander (cilantro)

**1** Preheat oven to 350°F.

**2** Cut bread into thin triangles; place on baking sheet. Bake about 8 minutes or until crisp.

**3** Meanwhile, combine juice, onion, and garlic in small frying pan; cook, stirring, until onion softens.

**4** Blend or process onion mixture with cumin, chickpeas, milk, and oil until smooth; stir in coriander. Serve hummus with the pita crisps.

prep + cook time 15 minutes
nutritional information per serving
170 calories; 30.9g carbohydrate; 5.7g fiber; 2.6g fat (0.3g saturated fat); 1mg cholesterol; 267mg sodium; 7.6g protein; low GI

# curried lamb pockets

2 cups all-purpose flour

1 cup whole wheat flour

⅓ cup polenta

1 tablespoon cumin seeds

4 ounces reduced-fat cream
    cheese, coarsely chopped

¾ cup warm water, approximately

2 tablespoons 1% low-fat milk,
    approximately

LAMB FILLING

8 ounces lean ground lamb

½ medium orange sweet potato,
    coarsely grated

1 small yellow onion (3 ounces),
    finely chopped

½ medium red bell pepper
    (3 ounces), finely chopped

2 teaspoons green curry paste

¼ cup beef stock

⅓ cup (1½ ounces) frozen peas

1 tablespoon finely chopped
    fresh mint

**1** Sift flours into large bowl, stir in
polenta and seeds; rub in cream
cheese until mixture is crumbly.
Stir in enough of the water to
make ingredients cling together.
Turn dough onto floured surface,
knead gently until smooth. Wrap
pastry in plastic wrap; refrigerate
30 minutes.

**2** Meanwhile, make lamb filling.

**3** Preheat oven to 400°F. Oil two
baking sheets.

**4** Roll out half the pastry between
sheets of parchment paper until
⅛-inch thick. Cut six 4¾-inch
rounds from pastry. Repeat with
remaining pastry.

**5** Place rounded tablespoons of
cold lamb filling in center
of each pastry round; brush edges
with a little milk. Fold in half,
press edges together to seal. Place
pockets about 2 inches apart on
baking sheets; brush with a little
extra milk. Bake about 25 minutes
or until pastry is browned lightly.

LAMB FILLING Spray a medium
frying pan with cooking spray,
place it over medium heat. Cook
the lamb, stirring, until browned.
Add sweet potato, onion, peppers,
and cook, stirring, until vegetables
soften. Add curry paste; cook,
stirring, until fragrant. Add stock
and peas; cook, stirring, about
3 minutes or until liquid has
evaporated. Remove from heat;
stir in mint. Cool.

prep + cook time 1 hour 25 minutes
(+ refrigeration)
nutritional information per pasty
220 calories; 30.3g carbohydrate;
2.7g fiber; 7.3g fat (3.3g saturated
fat); 21mg cholesterol; 66mg
sodium; 8.6g protein; low GI

LUNCHES & LIGHT MEALS 65

# tomato, bean, and pasta soup

serves 4

1 large yellow onion, finely
  chopped
1 cup reduced-sodium chicken
  stock
3 cups water
14-ounce can crushed tomatoes
1 teaspoon finely chopped fresh
  oregano
¾ cup (3 ounces) whole wheat
  pasta spirals
14-ounce can four-bean mix,
  rinsed, drained
2 medium zucchini (8 ounces),
  coarsely chopped
2 tablespoons coarsely chopped
  fresh flat-leaf parsley

**1** Cook onion and 2 tablespoons of the stock in large saucepan, stirring, until onion softens. Add remaining stock, the water, undrained tomatoes, and oregano; bring to a boil. Add pasta; boil, uncovered, 10 minutes.

**2** Add beans and zucchini; simmer, uncovered, about 5 minutes or until pasta is tender. Serve soup garnished with parsley; accompany with whole wheat bread, if you like.

prep + cook time 50 minutes
nutritional information per serving
224 calories; 44.8g carbohydrate; 9.6g fiber; 1.1g fat (0.2g saturated fat); 0mg cholesterol; 461mg sodium; 12.6g protein; low GI

# asparagus frittata with arugula

serves 2

1 small red onion (3 ounces), thinly sliced

6–8 large spears (6 ounces) asparagus, trimmed, coarsely chopped

2 large eggs

2 large egg whites

2 tablespoons low-fat cottage cheese

3 cups (1½ ounces) baby arugula leaves

2 tablespoons lemon juice

2 teaspoons rinsed, drained baby capers

**1** Preheat broiler.

**2** Spray small frying pan with cooking oil spray; cook onion over medium heat, stirring, 1 minute. Add asparagus; cook, stirring, 2 minutes.

**3** Combine eggs, egg whites, and cheese in a medium bowl. Pour over asparagus mixture in pan. Cook, uncovered, about 5 minutes or until frittata is browned underneath.

**4** Place pan under broiler about 5 minutes or until frittata is set.

**5** Combine remaining ingredients in medium bowl; serve frittata with salad.

prep + cook time 25 minutes
nutritional information per serving
139 calories; 8.8g carbohydrate; 2.8g fiber; 5.3g fat (1.8g saturated fat); 187mg cholesterol; 272mg sodium; 14.2g protein; low GI

tips If the handle of your frying pan is not heatproof, cover it with aluminium foil before placing it under the broiler.

Frittata is delicious served warm, but if you like it cold and want to take it to work, make it the evening before, keep it in the fridge overnight, then wrap it in plastic wrap the next morning.

# carrot and lentil soup with caraway toast

serves 6

1 cup vegetable stock
2 large yellow onions (14 ounces), finely chopped
2 cloves garlic, crushed
1 tablespoon ground cumin
6 large carrots (1 pound), coarsely chopped
2 stalks celery (5 ounces), trimmed, coarsely chopped
5½ cups water
½ cup brown lentils
½ cup 1% low-fat buttermilk

CARAWAY TOAST
6 slices whole wheat bread
⅓ cup (1 ounce) finely grated parmesan cheese
2 cloves garlic, crushed
1 teaspoon caraway seeds
2 tablespoons finely chopped fresh flat-leaf parsley

**1** Combine ½ cup of the stock, onion, garlic, and cumin in large saucepan over medium heat and cook, stirring, until onion softens. Add carrot and celery; cook, stirring, 5 minutes. Add remaining stock and the water; bring to a boil. Reduce heat; simmer, uncovered, about 20 minutes or until vegetables are tender. Cool mixture 10 minutes.
**2** Blend or process mixture, in batches, until smooth. Return mixture to pan; add lentils. Simmer, uncovered, about 20 minutes or until lentils are tender.
**3** Meanwhile, make caraway toast.
**4** Remove soup from heat; stir in buttermilk. Serve with the toast.

CARAWAY TOAST Preheat broiler. Place bread, in single layer, on baking sheet; cook under broiler until browned lightly on one side. Sprinkle combined cheese, garlic, seeds, and parsley over untoasted sides of bread; cook under broiler until browned lightly. Cut in half.

prep + cook time 1 hour 10 minutes
nutritional information per serving
234 calories; 40.5g carbohydrate; 8.2g fiber; 3.4g fat (1.0g saturated fat); 5mg cholesterol; 383mg sodium; 11.7g protein; medium GI

# spinach, tomato, and prosciutto whole grain pizza

serves 6

⅓ cup finely cracked buckwheat
¼ cup bulgur
¾ cup warm water
1 teaspoon superfine sugar
½-ounce packet dried yeast
1½ cups all-purpose flour
1 cup whole wheat flour
½ cup tomato pasta sauce
¾ cup (2½ ounces) coarsely grated reduced-fat mozzarella cheese
2 cups (8 ounces) red grape tomatoes, halved
6 slices prosciutto (3 ounces), coarsely chopped
2 cups (1½ ounces) baby spinach leaves, trimmed

**1** Combine buckwheat and bulgur in medium heatproof bowl; cover with boiling water. Cover, stand 30 minutes. Rinse under cold water; drain buckwheat mixture thoroughly.
**2** Combine the water, sugar, and yeast in small bowl. Stand in warm place about 10 minutes or until frothy.

**3** Combine buckwheat mixture in large bowl with flours. Add yeast mixture; mix to a soft dough. Knead dough on floured surface about 10 minutes or until smooth and elastic. Place dough in lightly oiled large bowl; cover. Stand in warm place about 1 hour or until doubled in size.
**4** Preheat oven to 425°F. Oil two pizza trays or baking sheets with cooking spray.
**5** Divide dough in half. Roll each portion on floured surface into 12-inch round; place one on each pan.
**6** Spread pizza crusts with sauce; sprinkle half the cheese over them, then top with tomato and prosciutto. Sprinkle the remaining cheese over pizzas. Bake about 20 minutes or until top is browned lightly and crusts are crisp. Serve pizzas topped with spinach.

prep + cook time 45 minutes (+ standing)
nutritional information per serving 329 calories; 56.0g carbohydrate; 6.7g fiber; 5.1g fat (1.9g saturated fat); 15mg cholesterol; 552mg sodium; 17.7g protein; medium GI

tip Serve with a green salad.

# ham, tomato, and arugula pizza   makes 2

2 large whole wheat pita breads

2 tablespoons no-added-salt tomato paste

4 ounces shaved low-sodium lean ham

1¾ cups (8 ounces) cherry tomatoes, halved

¼ small red onion (1 ounce), thinly sliced

⅓ cup (3 ounces) low-fat ricotta cheese

1½ cups (1 ounce) baby arugula leaves

2 tablespoons finely shredded fresh basil

**1** Preheat oven to 400°F.

**2** Place bread on baking sheets; spread paste over them. Divide ham, tomato, and onion between breads; top with dollops of cheese.

**3** Bake about 10 minutes. Serve pizza garnished with arugula and basil.

prep + cook time 25 minutes
nutritional information per pizza
317 calories; 48.7g carbohydrate; 7.7g fiber; 5.0g fat (1.6g saturated fat); 39mg cholesterol; 924mg sodium; 23.2g protein; medium GI

# chicken and bacon club sandwich

serves 2

3 ounces boneless skinless chicken breast

2 slices bacon (1 ounce)

⅓ cup low-fat cottage cheese

4 slices rye bread, toasted

1 cup (¾ ounce) baby arugula leaves

1 small tomato (3 ounces), thinly sliced

**1** Spray a small frying pan with cooking spray and heat over medium heat, add the chicken and cook through. Cover chicken; stand 5 minutes, then thinly slice.
**2** Cook bacon in same pan until crisp.
**3** Divide half the cheese between two toast slices; top with arugula, tomato, chicken, bacon, remaining cheese, and toast.

prep + cook time 20 minutes
nutritional information per serving
331 calories; 40.2g carbohydrate; 4.7g fiber; 10.1g fat (2.7g saturated fat); 40mg cholesterol; 651mg sodium; 23.3g protein; medium GI

tip This sandwich is at its best eaten warm, but if you can't cook the chicken and bacon at lunch time, cook them in the morning and assemble the sandwich at work.

# salmon pasta salad

1 cup spiral pasta

6–8 large spears (6 ounces) asparagus, trimmed, coarsely chopped

1 teaspoon finely grated lemon rind

¼ cup lemon juice

1 clove garlic, crushed

2 tablespoons low-fat ricotta cheese

1 medium red bell pepper (5 ounces), thinly sliced

⅓ cup coarsely chopped fresh flat-leaf parsley

2 scallions, thinly sliced

6 ounces canned unsalted pink salmon in springwater, drained, flaked

1 Cook pasta in medium saucepan of boiling water, uncovered, until tender. Add asparagus; cook 1 minute. Drain.

2 Meanwhile, combine rind, juice, and garlic in large bowl; add pasta, asparagus, and remaining ingredients to bowl; toss to combine.

prep + cook time 25 minutes
nutritional information per serving
348 calories; 40.3g carbohydrate; 4.5g fiber; 8.0g fat (2.1g saturated fat); 42mg cholesterol; 116mg sodium; 27.2g protein; low GI

tip Choose any pasta you like for this salad.

# main
# courses

# herb-stuffed chicken with tomato salad

serves 4

1¼ pounds fingerling potatoes

¼ cup finely chopped fresh basil

1 tablespoon finely chopped fresh oregano

2 teaspoons fresh lemon thyme leaves

2 cloves garlic, crushed

1 tablespoon finely grated lemon rind

4 x 4-ounce boneless, skinless chicken breasts

4 slices prosciutto (2 ounces)

1¾ cups (8 ounces) cherry tomatoes

1¾ cups (8 ounces) yellow cherry tomatoes

6 cups (4 ounces) baby spinach leaves

½ cup coarsely chopped fresh basil

2 tablespoons red wine vinegar

2 teaspoons olive oil

**1** Preheat oven to 425°F. Oil large baking dish with cooking spray.

**2** Halve unpeeled potatoes lengthwise. Place potato, in single layer, in dish; spray lightly with oil. Roast about 45 minutes or until browned lightly and tender.

**3** Meanwhile, combine finely chopped basil, oregano, thyme, garlic, and rind in small bowl. Halve chicken breasts horizontally, without cutting all the way through; open chicken breasts out flat onto board. Divide herb mixture among chicken pieces; fold to enclose filling, wrapping each with a prosciutto slice to secure.

**4** Spray a large frying pan with cooking spray, heat over medium heat, and cook chicken about 10 minutes or until browned all over; place chicken on baking sheet. Roast in oven during the last 15 minutes of the potato cooking time, or until chicken is cooked through.

**5** Meanwhile, cook tomatoes in same pan, over high heat, stirring, 3 minutes. Combine tomatoes, spinach, and coarsely chopped basil in large bowl with combined vinegar and oil. Serve salad with chicken and potatoes. Garnish chicken with extra lemon thyme leaves, if you like.

prep + cook time 1 hour 10 minutes
nutritional information per serving
331 calories; 34.2g carbohydrate; 6.0g fiber; 7.3g fat (1.6g saturated fat); 80mg cholesterol; 588mg sodium; 33.4g protein; medium GI

# chili coriander lamb and barley salad

serves 4

1 tablespoon coriander seeds, lightly crushed

½ teaspoon dried chili flakes

2 cloves garlic, crushed

1¼ pounds boneless lamb loin

1 cup pearl barley

¼ teaspoon ground turmeric

⅓ cup fresh mint leaves

⅓ cup fresh coriander leaves (cilantro)

1 small red onion (3 ounces), finely chopped

1½ cups (8 ounces) cherry tomatoes, halved

¼ cup lemon juice

2 teaspoons olive oil

1  Combine seeds, chili, and garlic in medium bowl, add lamb; toss to coat lamb in mixture. Cover, refrigerate 30 minutes.

2  Meanwhile, cook barley in large saucepan of boiling water, about 20 minutes or until barley is tender; drain. Rinse under cold water; drain.

3  Spray a stovetop grill pan with cooking spray (or oil a grill or barbecue) and heat to medium-high. Cook the lamb as desired, turning once. Cover lamb; stand 5 minutes, then slice thickly.

4  Meanwhile, combine remaining ingredients in large bowl, add barley; stir to combine. Serve barley salad with lamb.

prep + cook time 50 minutes (+ refrigeration)

nutritional information per serving 429 calories; 44.4g carbohydrate; 9.6g fiber; 11.8g fat (3.5g saturated fat); 94mg cholesterol; 106mg sodium; 35.6g protein; low GI

# linguine marinara

serves 4

4 ounces linguine pasta

12 ounces mixed seafood: shrimp, scallops, mussels

1 small yellow onion (3 ounces), finely chopped

2 cloves garlic, crushed

1 fresh small red Thai (serrano) chili, finely chopped

14-ounce can no-added-salt diced tomatoes

¼ cup water

⅓ cup coarsely chopped fresh flat-leaf parsley

**1** Cook pasta in large saucepan of boiling water until tender; drain.

**2** Meanwhile, spray a large skillet with cooking spray over medium-high heat. Add the seafood, cover, and cook until shrimp turns opaque and mussels open. Remove seafood from the pan.

**3** Add onion, garlic, and chili to same heated pan; cook, stirring, about 5 minutes or until onion softens. Add undrained tomatoes and the water; cook, stirring, 5 minutes. Return seafood to pan; cook, stirring occasionally, about 2 minutes or until heated through. Stir in parsley.

**4** Serve pasta topped with marinara sauce.

prep + cook time 20 minutes
nutritional information per serving
238 calories; 32.1g carbohydrate; 2.2g fiber; 2.3g fat (0.5g saturated fat); 63mg cholesterol; 471mg sodium; 21.5g protein; low GI

tip Don't overcook the seafood— if you do, it will become tough and leathery—or the pasta. Cooked pasta with a little bit of bite has a lower glycemic index.

# garlic shrimp and bok choy with herbed rice

serves 6

36 uncooked jumbo shrimp
   (2 pounds)
6 cloves garlic, crushed
2 teaspoons finely chopped fresh
   coriander (cilantro)
2 fresh small red Thai (serrano)
   chilies, finely chopped
1 teaspoon light brown sugar
⅓ cup lime juice
2 teaspoons peanut oil
2 pounds baby bok choy,
   quartered lengthwise
6 scallions, thinly sliced
1 tablespoon sweet chili sauce

HERBED RICE
2 cups long-grain brown rice
3 cups water
2 tablespoons coarsely chopped
   fresh coriander (cilantro)
1 tablespoon coarsely chopped
   fresh mint
1 tablespoon coarsely chopped
   fresh flat-leaf parsley
1 teaspoon finely grated lime rind

**1** Shell and devein shrimp,
leaving tails intact.
**2** Combine shrimp in large bowl
with garlic, coriander, chili, sugar,
and juice.
**3** Make herbed rice.
**4** Meanwhile, heat oil in wok over
medium-high heat; stir-fry
shrimp, in batches, until changed
in color. Remove from wok.

**5** Add bok choy, onion, sauce, and
shrimp marinade to wok; stir-fry
until bok choy is tender. Return
shrimp to wok; stir-fry until hot.
Serve shrimp and bok choy
mixture with herbed rice.

HERBED RICE Cook rice in large
saucepan of boiling water,
uncovered, about 30 minutes or
until tender; drain. Fluff rice with
fork. Stir in remaining ingredients.

prep + cook time 50 minutes
nutritional information per serving
371 calories; 50.8g carbohydrate;
3.2g fiber; 4.7g fat (0.5g saturated
fat); 191mg cholesterol; 1031mg
sodium; 27.1g protein; medium GI

tips Traditional garlic shrimp are
given a Southeast Asian tweak in
this recipe.

Bok choy has become as common
a vegetable staple as green beans
or broccoli in most kitchens; it's
versatile, easy to cook, keeps well,
and is delicious.

# moroccan kebabs with preserved lemon couscous

serves 4

½ cup finely chopped fresh coriander (cilantro)

2 cloves garlic, crushed

1 tablespoon olive oil

2 fresh small red Thai (serrano) chilies, finely chopped

¼ cup lemon juice

1¼ pounds skinless firm white fish filets, cut into 1¼-inch pieces

1 cup reduced-sodium chicken stock

½ cup water

1½ cups couscous

½ cup firmly packed fresh coriander leaves (cilantro)

1 tablespoon finely chopped preserved lemon rind

¼ cup toasted slivered almonds

**1** Combine chopped coriander, garlic, oil, chili, and juice in small bowl. Place half the coriander mixture in large bowl, add fish; toss to coat fish in mixture. Thread fish onto eight skewers; place kebabs on tray. Cover, refrigerate 45 minutes.

**2** Spray a stovetop grill pan with cooking spray (or oil a grill or barbecue) and heat to medium-high. Grill the kebabs, turning frequently, until cooked as desired, about 5 minutes.

**3** Meanwhile, bring stock and the water to a boil in medium saucepan; remove from heat. Add couscous to stock, cover; stand about 5 minutes or until liquid is absorbed, fluffing with fork occasionally. Add remaining coriander mixture, coriander leaves, lemon, and nuts to couscous; stir to combine. Serve couscous with kebabs.

prep + cook time 35 minutes (+ refrigeration)
nutritional information per serving
427 calories; 52.6g carbohydrate; 4.2g fiber; 8.1g fat (1.0g saturated fat); 54mg cholesterol; 223mg sodium; 33.0g protein; low GI

tips You will need to soak eight 10-inch bamboo skewers in water for at least an hour before using them to prevent them from burning during cooking.

Preserved lemons can be found in jars in Middle Eastern supermarkets or in the ethnic foods aisle of your local grocery store. To use preserved lemon rind, rinse well and discard the flesh, using the rind only.

Serve with an arugula or spinach salad.

# thai basil chicken stir-fry

serves 6

1 teaspoon sesame oil

¼ cup low-sodium soy sauce

¼ cup lime juice

2 tablespoons honey

2 fresh small red Thai (serrano) chilies, thinly sliced

2 teaspoons cornstarch

1¾ pounds chicken breast filets, thinly sliced

1½ cups long-grain brown rice

3 cups water

1 tablespoon peanut oil

3 cloves garlic, crushed

2 large red onions (14 ounces), thinly sliced

1½ cups (8 ounces) jarred baby corn ears

¼ cup water, extra

2 teaspoons finely grated lime rind

3 cups (8 ounces) bean sprouts

2 cups loosely packed fresh Thai basil leaves

1 cup loosely packed fresh coriander leaves (cilantro)

**1** Combine sesame oil, sauce, juice, honey, chili, and cornstarch in large bowl. Add chicken; toss to coat chicken in marinade. Cover, refrigerate 1 hour.

**2** Cook rice in a large saucepan of boiling water, uncovered, about 30 minutes, or until tender. Drain.

**3** Drain chicken through a strainer set over a bowl; reserve marinade.

**4** Heat half the peanut oil in wok over medium-high heat; stir-fry chicken, in batches, until browned all over. Remove from wok. Heat remaining peanut oil in wok; stir-fry garlic, onion, and corn until tender. Return chicken to wok with reserved marinade, the extra water, and rind; stir-fry until sauce boils and chicken is cooked.

**5** Remove from heat; add sprouts and herbs. Serve stir-fry with rice; accompany with lime wedges, if you like.

prep + cook time  40 minutes (+ refrigeration)

nutritional information per serving
445 calories; 55.0g carbohydrate; 4.0g fiber; 8.3g fat (1.4g saturated fat); 85mg cholesterol; 527mg sodium; 35.6g protein; medium GI

tips You need to grate the rind from the lime before you juice it.

Thai basil has slightly smaller leaves than sweet Italian basil, and a strong, somewhat aniseed, flavor.

# lime and chili fish baked in banana leaves

serves 8

2 large banana leaves

4 × 4-inch stalks fresh lemon grass

3 fresh small red Thai (serrano) chilies, thinly sliced

4 cloves garlic, crushed

1 tablespoon finely grated lime rind

⅓ cup lime juice

2 tablespoons finely grated fresh ginger

1 cup coarsely chopped fresh coriander (cilantro)

⅔ cup light coconut milk

8 × 4-ounce firm white fish filets

2½ cups long-grain brown rice

4 scallions, thinly sliced

**1** Preheat oven to 425°F.

**2** Trim each banana leaf into four 12-inch squares. Using metal tongs, dip one square at a time into large saucepan of boiling water; remove immediately. Rinse under cold running water; pat dry with paper towels. Banana leaf squares should be soft and pliable.

**3** Halve lemon grass lengthwise. Combine chili, garlic, rind, juice, ginger, coriander, and coconut milk in small bowl.

**4** Center each fish filet on banana leaf. Top with lemon grass; drizzle the chili mixture over each filet. Fold banana leaf over fish to enclose; secure each parcel with kitchen string.

**5** Cook rice in a large saucepan of boiling water, uncovered, about 30 minutes or until tender; drain. Stir in scallions.

**6** Meanwhile, place banana leaf parcels, in single layer, in large baking dish. Roast about 10 minutes or until fish is cooked as desired. Serve fish parcels with rice.

prep + cook time 50 minutes
nutritional information per serving
304 calories; 41.8g carbohydrate; 1.6g fiber; 3.3g fat (1.3g saturated fat); 43mg cholesterol; 72mg sodium; 21.9g protein; medium GI

tips Let your guests unwrap their own fish "package" at the table so the spicy aroma wafts up from the plates and awakens their appetites. Auminum foil can be used if banana leaves are unavailable. Many supermarkets and greengrocers sell bundles of trimmed banana-leaf squares; they can also be found frozen in specialty markets.

Fresh leaves can also be used as placemats for an Asian-themed meal.

# steaks with pepper salsa

serves 4

1¼ pounds fingering potatoes
1 medium red bell pepper
   (5 ounces), finely chopped
1 medium green bell pepper
   (5 ounces), finely chopped
1 medium red onion (6 ounces),
   finely chopped
1 large tomato (8 ounces), seeded,
   finely chopped
1 tablespoon coarsely chopped
   fresh coriander (cilantro)
¼ cup fat-free French dressing
2 cloves garlic, crushed
1 teaspoon ground cumin
4 x 4-ounce beef tenderloin steaks
3¼ cups (2 ounces) baby arugula
   leaves

**1** Preheat oven to 425°F. Oil large baking dish with cooking spray.
**2** Halve unpeeled potatoes lengthwise. Place potatoes, in single layer, in dish; spray lightly with oil. Roast about 45 minutes or until browned lightly and tender.
**3** Meanwhile, to make pepper salsa, combine peppers, onion, tomato, coriander, dressing, garlic, and cumin in medium bowl.
**4** Spray a grill pan with cooking spray (or oil a grill or barbecue) and heat to medium-high. Add the beef and cook until browned on both sides and to desired temperature. Cover beef; stand 5 minutes. Serve beef with pepper salsa, roasted potatoes, and arugula.

prep + cook time **1** hour
nutritional information per serving
282 calories; 36.4g carbohydrate;
5.3g fiber; 4.7g fat (1.6g saturated fat); 60mg cholesterol; 227mg sodium; 26.5g protein; medium GI

# shrimp and basil risotto

serves 4

1 pound uncooked medium shrimp

1 cup no-added-salt chicken stock

1 cup dry white wine

3 cups water

1 large stalk celery (2 ounces), trimmed, finely chopped

1 small yellow onion (3 ounces), finely chopped

1 cup arborio rice

1 cup cooked brown long-grain rice

2 medium tomatoes (10 ounces), seeded, finely chopped

½ cup loosely packed fresh basil leaves

2 tablespoons finely chopped fresh flat-leaf parsley

**1** Shell and devein shrimp, leaving tails intact.

**2** Bring stock, wine, and 2 cups of the water to a boil in medium saucepan. Reduce heat; simmer, covered.

**3** Meanwhile, cook celery, onion, and the remaining water in large saucepan over medium heat, stirring, about 10 minutes or until water has evaporated. Stir in arborio rice.

**4** Add ½ cup of the simmering stock mixture to rice mixture; cook, stirring, over low heat until liquid is absorbed. Continue adding stock mixture, in ½-cup batches, stirring until liquid is absorbed after each addition. Total cooking time should be about 35 minutes or until rice is tender.

**5** After last addition of stock mixture, add shrimp and brown rice; cook, stirring, until shrimp change in color. Remove from heat; stir in tomato and herbs.

prep + cook time 50 minutes
nutritional information per serving
384 calories; 56.6g carbohydrate; 4.3g fiber; 2.7g fat (0.4g saturated fat); 149mg cholesterol; 702mg sodium; 23.0g protein; medium GI

*tip* You need to cook about ½ cup brown long-grain rice for this recipe.

# lentil patties with spicy eggplant sauce

serves 8

2 potatoes (12 ounces), chopped

⅔ cup red lentils

1 red bell pepper (4 ounces)

2 teaspoons olive oil

1 medium yellow onion (4 ounces), finely chopped

2 cloves garlic, crushed

2 tablespoons water

1 large stalk celery (2 ounces), trimmed, finely chopped

6 ounces medium swiss chard leaves, trimmed and shredded

¼ cup toasted pine nuts, chopped

1½ cups stale whole wheat bread crumbs

2 teaspoons coarsely chopped fresh coriander (cilantro)

1 tablespoon coarsely chopped fresh flat-leaf parsley

½ cup packaged bread crumbs

2 teaspoons vegetable oil

SPICY EGGPLANT SAUCE

1 large eggplant (18 ounces)

1 clove garlic, crushed

2 tablespoons lemon juice

1 tablespoon sweet chili sauce

¼ cup plain low-fat yogurt

1 tablespoon coarsely chopped fresh flat-leaf parsley

**1** Make spicy eggplant sauce.

**2** Meanwhile, boil, steam, or microwave potatoes until tender; drain. Mash potatoes until smooth.

**3** Cook lentils in medium saucepan of boiling water, about 8 minutes or until tender; drain.

**4** Preheat broiler to high. Quarter and seed peppers and roast under broiler, skin-side-up, until blackened. Transfer to plastic bag and rest 5 minutes; peel skin and coarsely chop.

**5** Heat olive oil in medium frying pan over medium heat; cook onion and garlic, stirring, until softened. Add the water and celery; cook, stirring, until water has almost evaporated. Add swiss chard; cook, stirring, until wilted.

**6** Combine mashed potatoes, lentils, peppers, onion mixture, pine nuts, stale bread crumbs, and herbs in bowl. Shape mixture into eight patties; toss in packaged bread crumbs, place on tray. Cover, refrigerate 1 hour.

**7** Heat vegetable oil in large frying pan over medium heat; cook patties about 2 minutes each side or until browned and heated through. Serve patties with spicy eggplant sauce.

SPICY EGGPLANT SAUCE Preheat oven to 350°F. Halve eggplant lengthwise and roast, cut-side down, on oiled baking sheet, until soft, about 45 minutes; cool. Scoop flesh and blend with garlic, juice, sauce, and yogurt. Stir in parsley.

prep + cook time 1 hour 30 minutes (+ refrigeration)
nutritional information per serving 264 calories; 45.0g carbohydrate; 10.3g fiber; 5.3g fat (0.6g saturated fat); 0.5mg cholesterol; 213mg sodium; 11.0g protein; medium GI

# tofu and spinach stir-fry

serves 4

8 ounces firm tofu

2 tablespoons hoisin sauce

1 tablespoon oyster sauce

1 tablespoon reduced-sodium soy sauce

1 teaspoon finely grated fresh ginger

2 cloves garlic, crushed

2 teaspoons peanut oil

1 large yellow onion (6 ounces), thinly sliced

1 large red bell pepper (6 ounces), thinly sliced

7 ounces (about 3 cups) snow peas

9 cups (10 ounces) spinach, trimmed, coarsely chopped

¼ cup water

8 ounces fresh egg noodles

**1** Cut tofu into ¾-inch cubes; spread, in single layer, on tray lined with paper towels. Cover tofu with more paper towel; stand 10 minutes.

**2** Combine sauces, ginger, garlic, and tofu in medium bowl. Cover, refrigerate 2 hours.

**3** Heat oil in wok over medium heat; stir-fry onion and peppers until onion softens. Add snow peas, spinach, the water, and tofu mixture; stir-fry until spinach wilts.

**4** Meanwhile, bring a pot of water to a boil; stir in noodles and cook until tender, 3 to 4 minutes or according to package instructions. Drain.

**5** Divide noodles among serving bowls, top with tofu and vegetable mixture.

prep + cook time 25 minutes (+ refrigeration)

nutritional information per serving 326 calories; 48.2g carbohydrate; 6.7g fiber; 8.1g fat (1.0g saturated fat); 41mg cholesterol; 501mg sodium; 16.1g protein; low GI

# eggplant, tomato, and leek lasagna

serves 6

3 medium eggplants (2 pounds)

1 large yellow onion (6 ounces), finely chopped

4 cloves garlic, crushed

3 large tomatoes (1¼ pounds), coarsely chopped

2 tablespoons no-added-salt tomato paste

¼ cup finely shredded fresh basil

½ cup water

2 teaspoons olive oil

2 medium leeks (1 pound), thinly sliced

1 tablespoon light brown sugar

4 ounces no-boil lasagna noodles

1 cup (4 ounces) coarsely grated reduced-fat cheddar cheese

**1** Heat a stovetop grill pan over medium-high. Spray with cooking spray. Slice eggplants lengthwise into ½-inch thick slices. Cook, in batches, until lightly browned and tender.

**2** Spray a medium frying pan with cooking spray; heat over medium heat and cook the onion and half the garlic, stirring, until softened. Stir in tomatoes, paste, and basil; bring to a boil, stirring. Reduce heat, simmer, uncovered, about 10 minutes or until sauce thickens. Cool 10 minutes, then blend or process tomato mixture with the water until almost smooth.

**3** Heat oil in same cleaned pan; cook leeks and remaining garlic, stirring, until softened. Add sugar; cook, stirring, about 5 minutes or until browned lightly.

**4** Preheat oven to 400°F. Oil deep 8-inch x 12-inch ovenproof dish.

**5** Arrange lasagna noodles to cover base of dish; top with a quarter of the eggplant, a quarter of the leek mixture, a quarter of the tomato mixture, and a quarter of the cheese. Repeat to make three layers. Bake about 50 minutes. Stand 10 minutes before serving.

prep + cook time 1 hour
nutritional information per serving
263 calories; 44.1g carbohydrate; 12.3g fiber; 6.1g fat (2.6g saturated fat); 11mg cholesterol; 159mg sodium; 12.3g protein; low GI

tip Serve with a garden salad.

# chicken and squash curry

½ cup brown long-grain rice

1 small red onion (3 ounces), finely chopped

2 tablespoons finely chopped coriander (cilantro) roots and stems

¼ cup firmly packed fresh coriander leaves (cilantro)

2 fresh long red chilies, coarsely chopped

2 cloves garlic, crushed

2-inch piece fresh ginger (1 ounce), finely grated

1 teaspoon ground turmeric

1 cup reduced-sodium chicken stock

6 ounces chicken breast filet, thinly sliced

¼ cup light coconut milk

4 ounces butternut squash, diced (about 1 cup)

1 cup (4 ounces) baby corn ears, coarsely chopped

1 cup (3 ounces) bean sprouts

2 tablespoons fresh coriander leaves (cilantro), extra

**1** Cook rice in large saucepan of boiling water until tender; drain.

**2** Meanwhile, blend onion, coriander roots and stems, coriander leaves, chili, garlic, ginger, and turmeric until a smooth paste forms.

**3** Cook paste in medium saucepan over medium heat, stirring, until fragrant. Add stock, chicken, and coconut milk; bring to a boil. Reduce heat; simmer, covered, 10 minutes.

**4** Add squash and corn to pan; simmer, uncovered, about 10 minutes or until squash is tender.

**5** Serve rice topped with curry, sprouts, and extra coriander.

prep + cook time 45 minutes
nutritional information per serving
226 calories; 35.1g carbohydrate; 3.3g fiber; 3.3g fat (1.2g saturated fat); 27mg cholesterol; 172mg sodium; 13.9g protein; medium GI

tips Brown rice takes about 30 minutes to cook, sometimes less depending on how crunchy you like it.

Any leftover curry will taste just as good if reheated in a microwave oven the next day.

# pumpkin and split pea tagine

serves 6

1 cup green split peas

1 tablespoon olive oil

1 medium yellow onion (4 ounces), finely chopped

2 cloves garlic, crushed

2 teaspoons ground coriander

2 teaspoons ground cumin

2 teaspoons ground ginger

1 teaspoon sweet paprika

1 teaspoon ground allspice

2 pounds pumpkin, cut into 1¼-inch pieces

14-ounce can crushed tomatoes

1 cup water

1 cup vegetable stock

2 tablespoons honey

6 ounces (about 2 cups) green beans, trimmed, coarsely chopped

¼ cup coarsely chopped fresh coriander (cilantro)

**1** Cook split peas in medium saucepan of boiling water, until tender; drain. Rinse under cold water; drain.

**2** Meanwhile, heat oil in large saucepan over medium heat; cook onion, stirring, until softened. Add garlic and spices; cook, stirring, about 2 minutes or until fragrant. Add pumpkin; stir to coat pumpkin in spice mixture.

**3** Stir in undrained tomatoes, the water and stock; bring to a boil. Reduce heat; simmer, uncovered, about 20 minutes or until pumpkin is tender. Stir in honey, beans, and split peas; simmer, uncovered, about 5 minutes or until beans are tender. Remove from heat; stir in coriander.

prep + cook time 55 minutes
nutritional information per serving 238 calories; 44.3 carbohydrate; 11.4g fiber; 3.4g fat (0.5g saturated fat); 0mg cholesterol; 212mg sodium; 10.8g protein; medium GI

tip Serve with steamed couscous.

# brown rice pilaf

serves 4

1 medium sweet potato (6 ounces), coarsely chopped

½ cup vegetable stock

1 cup water

2 teaspoons olive oil

1 medium yellow onion (4 ounces), finely chopped

2 cloves garlic, crushed

2 stalks celery (5 ounces), trimmed, thinly sliced

7-ounce package button mushrooms, halved

¾ cup brown medium-grain rice

1 tablespoon finely grated lemon rind

½ cup loosely packed fresh flat-leaf parsley leaves

**1** Preheat oven to 350°F.

**2** Place potato on parchment-paper-lined baking sheet; spray lightly with cooking spray. Roast about 25 minutes or until tender.

**3** Meanwhile, place stock and the water in small saucepan; bring to a boil. Reduce heat; simmer, covered.

**4** Heat oil in medium saucepan over medium heat; cook onion, garlic, and celery, stirring, until onion softens. Add mushrooms and rice; cook, stirring, 2 minutes. Add stock, reduce heat; simmer, covered, about 50 minutes or until stock is absorbed and rice is tender. Stir in sweet potatoes, rind, and parsley.

prep + cook time 1 hour 15 minutes
nutritional information per serving
216 calories; 40.8g carbohydrate; 4.5g fiber; 3.7g fat (0.6g saturated fat); 0mg cholesterol; 106mg sodium; 5.2g protein; medium GI

# chicken, lentil, and spinach pasta  serves 6

2 teaspoons olive oil

1 small yellow onion (3 ounces), finely chopped

2 cloves garlic, crushed

4 ounces lean ground chicken

½ cup red lentils

2 cups reduced-sodium chicken stock

¾ cup water

2 tablespoons no-salt-added tomato paste

12 cups (8 ounces) baby spinach leaves

8 ounces shell pasta

**1** Heat oil in medium saucepan over medium heat; cook onion and garlic, stirring, until onion softens. Add chicken; cook, stirring, until browned. Stir in lentils, stock, the water, and paste; bring to a boil. Reduce heat; simmer, uncovered, about 10 minutes or until lentils are tender. Add spinach; stir until wilted.

**2** Meanwhile, cook pasta in large saucepan of boiling water, until tender; drain.

**3** Combine pasta and chicken sauce in large bowl.

prep + cook time 35 minutes
nutritional information per serving
275 calories; 45.4g carbohydrate; 6.4g fiber; 4.0g fat (0.8g saturated fat); 16mg cholesterol; 282mg sodium; 15.2g protein; low GI

# pasta primavera with poached salmon

serves 4

8 ounces fettuccine pasta

5 cups water

14 ounces skin-on salmon filets

6 black peppercorns

2 sprigs fresh dill

2 teaspoons finely grated lemon rind

2 teaspoons olive oil

2 cloves garlic, crushed

1 medium red onion (6 ounces), thinly sliced

8–10 large spears (6 ounces) asparagus, halved crosswise

½ cup frozen peas

4 ounces (about 2 cups) snow peas, trimmed, halved

2 tablespoons lemon juice

2 teaspoons finely chopped fresh dill

2 tablespoons coarsely chopped fresh flat-leaf parsley

**1** Cook pasta in large saucepan of boiling water until tender; drain.
**2** Meanwhile, combine the water, fish, peppercorns, dill sprigs, and half the rind in large saucepan; bring to a boil. Reduce heat; simmer, uncovered, 8 minutes, turning fish halfway through cooking time.
**3** Remove fish from poaching liquid; discard liquid. When cool enough to handle, remove and discard skin; flake fish into medium bowl.
**4** Heat oil in same cleaned pan over medium heat; cook garlic, onion, and asparagus, stirring, until asparagus is tender. Add peas, snow peas, juice, pasta, remaining rind, and fish; stir until hot. Remove from heat; stir in herbs.

prep + cook time 40 minutes
nutritional information per serving
439 calories; 51.8g carbohydrate; 4.9g fiber; 10.6g fat (1.7g saturated fat); 63mg cholesterol; 87mg sodium; 33.4g protein; low GI

tip Salmon is richer than tuna in essential omega-3 fatty acids. When going for omega-3s you can also boost intakes with fortified foods, just look on the label for the terms DHA or EPA, which describe the best form of omega fats.

# lemon chili pork with italian brown rice salad

serves 4

2 teaspoons finely grated lemon rind

2 tablespoons lemon juice

½ teaspoon dried chili flakes

2 teaspoons olive oil

4 x 7-ounce pork cutlets

ITALIAN BROWN RICE SALAD

1 cup brown long-grain rice

1 large red bell pepper (6 ounces), finely chopped

½ cup (2 ounces) pitted black olives, coarsely chopped

2 tablespoons rinsed, drained capers

½ cup coarsely chopped fresh basil

⅓ cup coarsely chopped fresh flat-leaf parsley

2 tablespoons lemon juice

2 teaspoons olive oil

**1** Combine rind, juice, chili, oil, and pork in medium bowl. Cover, refrigerate for 2 hours.

**2** Meanwhile, make Italian brown rice salad.

**3** Spray a stovetop grill pan with cooking spray (or oil a grill or barbecue) and heat over medium heat. Grill the pork until browned on both sides and cooked as desired. Cover pork; stand 5 minutes. Serve with rice salad.

ITALIAN BROWN RICE SALAD
Cook rice in large saucepan of boiling water until tender; drain. Rinse under cold water; drain. Combine rice and remaining ingredients in large bowl.

prep + cook time 1 hour 10 minutes (+ refrigeration)
nutritional information per serving
491 calories; 36.3g carbohydrate; 2.8g fiber; 17.8g fat (3.9g saturated fat); 116mg cholesterol; 333mg sodium; 41.0g protein; medium GI

tip Serve with an arugula or spinach salad.

# chili con carne

⅓ cup brown long-grain rice

1 small yellow onion (3 ounces), finely chopped

1 clove garlic, crushed

6 ounces lean ground beef

1 teaspoon ground cumin

1 teaspoon dried chili flakes

14-ounce can diced tomatoes

2 tablespoons no-salt-added tomato paste

½ cup water

½ cup canned four-bean mix, rinsed, drained

2 tablespoons low-fat plain yogurt

¼ cup coarsely chopped fresh flat-leaf parsley

**1** Cook rice in medium saucepan of boiling water until tender; drain.

**2** Meanwhile, spray a medium frying pan with cooking spray and place over medium heat. Add onions and garlic, stirring, until onion softens. Add beef and spices; cook, stirring, until beef is browned.

**3** Add undrained tomatoes, paste, and the water; bring to a boil. Reduce heat; simmer, covered, 10 minutes. Uncover; simmer about 10 minutes or until mixture thickens slightly. Stir in beans.

**4** Serve chili con carne and rice topped with yogurt. Garnish with parsley.

prep + cook time 40 minutes
nutritional information per serving
352 calories; 49.5g carbohydrate; 6.8g fiber; 5.3g fat (1.7g saturated fat); 46mg cholesterol; 477mg sodium; 25.9g protein; medium GI

tip This is a great recipe (both the rice and the meat mixture) to cook in large batches, ready to freeze in user-friendly portions.

# seared tuna with chilled soba

serves 4

6 ounces dried soba noodles
¼ cup mirin
2 tablespoons kecap manis
1 tablespoon cooking sake
2 teaspoons white sugar
2-inch piece fresh ginger
    (1 ounce), finely grated
1 clove garlic, crushed
4 tuna steaks (5 ounces each)
1 sheet toasted seaweed
    (yaki-nori), thinly sliced
2 scallions, finely chopped
1 teaspoon sesame oil
2 tablespoons pickled ginger,
    thinly sliced

**1** Cook noodles in large saucepan of boiling water, until tender; drain. Rinse under cold water; drain. Place noodles in medium bowl; cover, refrigerate until needed.
**2** Meanwhile, combine mirin, kecap manis, sake, sugar, fresh ginger, and garlic in small bowl.

**3** Spray a large frying pan with cooking spray and place over high heat. Sear the tuna for 30 seconds on each side, until browned. Add the mirin mixture to the pan; coat fish on both sides in mixture. Remove fish from pan; cover to keep warm.
**4** Bring mixture in pan to a boil. Reduce heat; simmer, uncovered, 30 seconds. Strain sauce into small bowl.
**5** Meanwhile, combine nori, scallions, oil, and pickled ginger in bowl with noodles. Divide fish among plates, drizzle the sauce over it; top with noodle mixture. Serve with wasabi paste, if you like.

prep + cook time 25 minutes
nutritional information per serving
379 calories; 41.2g carbohydrate; 2.7g fiber; 3.7g fat (0.7g saturated fat); 67mg cholesterol; 464mg sodium; 37.6g protein; medium GI

# pasta with tomatoes, artichokes, and olives

serves 6

2 teaspoons olive oil

1 medium yellow onion (5 ounces), finely chopped

2 cloves garlic, crushed

¼ cup dry white wine

2 x 14-ounce cans no-salt-added crushed tomatoes

2 tablespoons no-salt-added tomato paste

⅓ cup (1½ ounces) pitted black olives

14-ounce can artichoke hearts in brine, drained, quartered

2 tablespoons coarsely chopped fresh basil

8 ounces whole wheat spiral pasta

⅓ cup (1 ounce) finely grated parmesan cheese

**1** Heat oil in medium saucepan over medium heat; cook onion and garlic, stirring, until onion softens. Add wine, undrained tomatoes, and paste; bring to a boil. Reduce heat; simmer, uncovered, about 15 minutes or until sauce has thickened. Add olives, artichokes, and basil; stir until heated through.

**2** Meanwhile, cook pasta in large saucepan of boiling water, until tender; drain.

**3** Combine pasta and sauce in large bowl. Serve pasta topped with cheese.

prep + cook time 40 minutes
nutritional information per serving
274 calories; 43.6g carbohydrate; 8.6g fiber; 8.8g fat (1.2g saturated fat); 3mg cholesterol; 341mg sodium; 8.8g protein; low GI

# veal and fennel rolls with horseradish mashed potatoes

serves 4

2 teaspoons olive oil

2 cloves garlic, crushed

2 small fennel bulbs (14 ounces), thinly sliced

3 portobello mushrooms (8 ounces), thickly sliced

½ cup dry white wine

1 cup water

6 boneless veal steaks (3 ounces each)

2 tablespoons whole wheat flour

½ cup chicken stock

1 tablespoon finely chopped fresh flat-leaf parsley

HORSERADISH MASHED POTATOES

1¼ pounds potatoes, coarsely chopped

1 tablespoon prepared jarred horseradish

¾ cup 1% low-fat milk, heated

2 tablespoons finely chopped fresh flat-leaf parsley

**1** Heat half the oil in large frying pan over medium heat; cook garlic and fennel, stirring, until fennel softens. Add mushrooms, half the wine, and ½ cup of the water; bring to a boil. Reduce heat; simmer, uncovered, about 15 minutes or until liquid has evaporated. Cool 10 minutes.

**2** Meanwhile, using meat mallet, gently pound veal steaks, one at a time, between pieces of plastic wrap until about ¼-inch thick; cut each piece in half crosswise. Divide fennel mixture among veal pieces; roll to enclose filling, secure each roll with a toothpick.

**3** Make horseradish mashed potatoes.

**4** Toss veal rolls in flour; shake off excess. Heat remaining oil in same cleaned frying pan over medium heat; cook rolls, in batches, until browned all over and cooked as desired. Remove from pan, cover to keep warm. Add remaining wine and water to same pan with stock; bring to a boil, stirring. Boil, uncovered, 5 minutes.

**5** Serve veal with mashed potatoes and sauce; garnish with parsley.

HORSERADISH MASHED POTATOES
Boil, steam, or microwave the potatoes; drain. Mash potatoes in large bowl; stir in horseradish and hot milk, then parsley.

prep + cook time 1 hour 10 minutes
nutritional information per serving
380 calories; 40.0g carbohydrate; 6.2g fiber; 7.3g fat (1.5g saturated fat); 112mg cholesterol; 334mg sodium; 33.4g protein; medium GI

tip Serve with a green salad or steamed green beans.

# whole wheat beet and goat cheese pizzas

makes 4

¼ cup cracked buckwheat
½ cup warm water
½ teaspoon superfine sugar
1 teaspoon dried yeast
¾ cup all-purpose flour
¾ cup whole wheat flour
2 large beets (14 ounces)
8 shallots (7 ounces), peeled
½ cup tomato paste
4 ounces goat cheese, crumbled
2½ cups (1½ ounces) baby
   arugula leaves

**1** Place buckwheat in small heatproof bowl; cover with boiling water. Stand 30 minutes, covered. Rinse under cold water; drain.
**2** Combine the water, sugar, and yeast in small bowl, cover; stand in a warm place about 10 minutes or until frothy.
**3** Combine buckwheat and sifted flours in large bowl. Add yeast mixture; mix to a soft dough. Knead dough on floured surface about 10 minutes or until smooth and elastic. Place dough in oiled large bowl. Cover; stand in warm place about 45 minutes or until doubled in size.
**4** Meanwhile, preheat oven to 425°F. Oil two large baking sheets.
**5** Trim leaves from beets, wrap unpeeled beets in foil; place in small shallow baking dish. Roast beets 20 minutes. Add shallots to dish; roast shallots with beets an additional 30 minutes or until

vegetables are tender. Cool 10 minutes. Peel beets; chop coarsely. Cut shallots into small wedges.
**6** Divide dough into four pieces. Roll each piece into 6-inch rounds; place on pans.
**7** Bake pizza crusts 10 minutes. Remove from oven; spread tomato paste on crusts, sprinkle the cheese over the crusts. Bake crusts about 8 minutes or until crisp.
**8** Top pizzas with beets, shallots, and arugula.

prep + cook time 50 minutes (+ standing)
nutritional information per pizza
372 calories; 64.9g carbohydrate; 8.1g fiber; 7.3g fat (4.3g saturated fat); 13mg cholesterol; 268mg sodium; 16.3g protein; medium GI

tip Wear disposable gloves when handling cooked beets. When you squeeze the warm beets, the skin will burst and peel away easily.

# brown fried rice with omelette

serves 4

1 cup brown long-grain rice

1 tablespoon peanut oil

3 large eggs, beaten lightly

2 cloves garlic, crushed

1-inch piece fresh ginger
(½ ounce), finely grated

1 fresh long red chili, finely
chopped

1 small red bell pepper (5 ounces),
cut into ½-inch pieces

4 ounces jarred baby corn, cut
into ½-inch pieces

3 ounces (about 1 cup) green
beans, trimmed, cut into
½-inch pieces

6–8 whole (3 ounces) fresh
shiitake mushrooms,
thinly sliced

2 tablespoons reduced-sodium
soy sauce

2 tablespoons rice vinegar

½ cup (2 ounces) bean sprouts,
trimmed

4 scallions, thinly sliced

**1** Cook rice in large saucepan of boiling water, until tender; drain. Cool.

**2** Heat half the oil in wok over medium heat; pour in half the egg, tilt wok to coat with egg. Cook until omelette is set. Remove omelette; roll tightly. Repeat with remaining egg. Thinly slice omelettes.

**3** Heat remaining oil in wok over medium-high heat; stir-fry garlic, ginger, and chili until fragrant. Add vegetables and stir-fry until tender.

**4** Add rice, sauce, vinegar, and sprouts; stir-fry until hot. Stir in half the scallions.

**5** Serve rice topped with remaining scallions and omelette strips.

prep + cook time 45 minutes
(+ cooling)
nutritional information per serving
333 calories; 49.7g carbohydrate;
4.7g fiber; 8.8g fat (1.8g saturated
fat); 140mg cholesterol; 412mg
sodium; 12.1g protein; medium GI

tip Rice can be cooked the
day before; store, covered,
in the fridge.

# grilled lamb chops with pumpkin risoni salad

serves 4

1 clove garlic, crushed

1 tablespoon finely chopped fresh oregano

1 tablespoon finely chopped fresh chives

2 tablespoons lemon juice

¼ cup dry white wine

12 French-trimmed lamb chops (1½ pounds)

PUMPKIN RISONI SALAD

1 pound pumpkin, peeled and cut into 1¼-inch pieces

1 clove garlic, crushed

1 tablespoon olive oil

1 cup risoni pasta

4 ounces baby spinach leaves

2 tablespoons lemon juice

2 tablespoons coarsely chopped fresh chives

2 tablespoons fresh oregano leaves

**1** Combine garlic, oregano, chives, juice, and wine in large bowl, add lamb; toss lamb to coat in marinade. Cover, refrigerate 1 hour.

**2** Meanwhile, make pumpkin risoni salad.

**3** Drain lamb; discard marinade. Spray a stovetop grill pan with cooking spray (or oil a grill or barbecue) and heat to medium-high. Cook the lamb chops, turning once, until charred and cooked to desired doneness. Serve cutlets with salad.

PUMPKIN RISONI SALAD  Preheat oven to 400°F. Place pumpkin, in single layer, on baking sheet; sprinkle the garlic and half the oil over it. Roast about 20 minutes or until tender. Meanwhile, cook pasta in large saucepan of boiling water until tender; drain. Combine pasta and spinach in large bowl with pumpkin, juice, herbs, and remaining oil.

prep + cook time 50 minutes (+ refrigeration)

nutritional information per serving 435 calories; 54.3g carbohydrate; 4.4g fiber; 10.1g fat (2.8g saturated fat); 62mg cholesterol; 136mg sodium; 29.6g protein; low GI

*tips* Risoni is a small rice-shaped pasta very similar to orzo; you can use either for this recipe.

Serve with steamed green beans and crusty whole wheat bread.

# fish and oven-roasted chips

serves 4

5 small potatoes (1⅓ pounds)
1 teaspoon sea salt
½ teaspoon cracked black pepper
4 x 4-ounce firm white fish filets
2 tablespoons rinsed, drained baby capers
1 tablespoon finely chopped fresh dill
1 teaspoon finely grated lemon rind
⅓ cup lemon juice
1 medium lemon, cut into wedges

CITRUS SALAD
1 medium orange (8 ounces), peeled, segmented
1 Lebanese cucumber (4 ounces), coarsely chopped
2½ cups (1½ ounces) baby spinach leaves
2½ cups (1½ ounces) baby arugula leaves
1 tablespoon white wine vinegar

**1** Preheat oven to 425°F. Oil large baking dish with cooking oil spray.
**2** Halve unpeeled potatoes lengthwise; cut each half into six wedges. Combine potatoes, in single layer, in dish with salt and pepper; spray lightly with cooking spray. Roast about 45 minutes or until browned lightly and tender.
**3** Meanwhile, make citrus salad.
**4** Spray a large frying pan with oil and heat over medium-high heat. Cook fish until browned both sides and cooked through.
**5** Drizzle the combined capers, dill, rind, and juice over the fish; serve with chips, citrus salad, and lemon wedges.

CITRUS SALAD Combine ingredients in medium bowl.

prep + cook time 55 minutes
nutritional information per serving
237 calories; 35.3g carbohydrate; 7.5g fiber; 1.0g fat (0.2g saturated fat); 43mg cholesterol; 560mg sodium; 22.3g protein; medium GI

tip We used bream filets in this recipe but you can use other firm white fish, such as whiting or tilapia.

# beef fajitas

1¼ pounds beef rump steak

16 x 6-inch flour tortillas

1 large red bell pepper (6 ounces), thinly sliced

1 large green bell pepper (6 ounces), thinly sliced

1 large yellow bell pepper (6 ounces), thinly sliced

1 large red onion (6 ounces), thinly sliced

3 cups finely shredded iceberg lettuce

1 cup (4 ounces) coarsely grated reduced-fat cheddar cheese

FRESH TOMATO SALSA

3 medium tomatoes (1 pound), seeded, finely chopped

1 medium red onion (6 ounces), finely chopped

1 tablespoon finely chopped drained pickled jalapeño chilies

¼ cup finely chopped fresh coriander (cilantro)

1 tablespoon lemon juice

**1** Preheat oven to 350°F.

**2** Make fresh tomato salsa.

**3** Spray a stovetop grill pan with cooking spray (or oil a grill or barbecue) and heat on high heat. Cook the beef, turning once, until desired doneness. Cover beef; stand 10 minutes, then thinly slice.

**4** Wrap tortillas in foil; heat in oven about 10 minutes or until warmed through.

**5** Meanwhile, cook peppers and onions on same grill pan, until vegetables are tender.

**6** Divide beef, peppers, and onions among tortillas. Top with lettuce, cheese, and fresh tomato salsa; roll to enclose filling.

FRESH TOMATO SALSA Combine ingredients in medium bowl.

prep + cook time 50 minutes
nutritional information per serving
345 calories; 38.1g carbohydrate; 4.5g fiber; 10.8g fat (4.1g saturated fat); 51mg cholesterol; 285mg sodium; 24.8g protein; low GI

tip You need a small head of iceberg lettuce for this recipe.

# warm pasta and lamb salad

1 pound lamb loin filets
⅓ cup lemon juice
2 tablespoons finely chopped
    fresh rosemary
1 tablespoon dry red wine
1 tablespoon sweet chili sauce
1 teaspoon light brown sugar
1 clove garlic, crushed
1 tablespoon olive oil
4 medium plum tomatoes
    (10 ounces), quartered
8 ounces whole wheat spiral pasta
½ cup reduced-sodium beef stock
2 tablespoons coarsely chopped
    fresh flat-leaf parsley
1 pound spinach, trimmed,
    coarsely chopped

**1** Combine lamb, juice, rosemary, wine, sauce, sugar, garlic, and half the oil in medium bowl. Cover, refrigerate 2 hours.
**2** Preheat oven to 350°F. Oil a baking sheet.
**3** Place tomatoes, in single layer, on pan. Bake about 20 minutes.
**4** Cook pasta in large saucepan of boiling water, until tender; drain.
**5** Meanwhile, drain lamb over medium bowl; reserve marinade. Heat remaining oil in medium frying pan over medium-high heat; cook lamb until browned and cooked as desired. Cover lamb; stand 5 minutes, then thinly slice.
**6** Add reserved marinade, stock, and parsley to same pan; bring to a boil.
**7** Combine tomato, pasta, lamb, marinade mixture, and spinach in large bowl.

prep + cook time 50 minutes
(+ refrigeration)
nutritional information per serving
453 calories; 52.1g carbohydrate; 8.2g fiber; 12g fat (3.8g saturated fat); 73mg cholesterol; 361mg sodium; 36.4g protein; low GI

# desserts

# cherry upside-down cakes

*makes 12*

15-ounce can pitted black
   cherries, drained

2 large eggs

¾ cup firmly packed light
   brown sugar

¾ cup ground almonds

1 teaspoon vanilla extract

⅓ cup whole wheat self-rising
   flour

½ cup 1% low-fat milk

**1** Preheat oven to 350°F. Grease
12-hole ⅓-cup muffin pan. Divide
cherries among pan holes.

**2** Beat eggs and sugar in small
bowl with electric mixer until
light and fluffy. Stir in ground
almonds, extract, flour, and milk.
Divide mixture evenly in the
muffin pan.

**3** Bake about 20 minutes. Stand
cakes 5 minutes before turning
out onto wire rack to cool.

prep + cook time **40 minutes**
nutritional information per cake
153 calories; 26.4g carbohydrate;
1.5g fiber; 4.4g fat (0.6g saturated
fat); 32mg cholesterol; 69mg
sodium; 3.9g protein; medium GI

# cranberry macerated berries

serves 4

8 ounces (about 2 cups) strawberries, quartered

4 ounces (about 1 cup) fresh raspberries

4 ounces (about 1 cup) fresh blueberries

1 tablespoon confectioners' sugar

½ cup apple, cranberry, and pomegranate juice

2 teaspoons finely grated orange rind

½ cup (4 ounces) low-fat vanilla-flavored yogurt

**1** Combine berries, sifted confectioners' sugar, juice, and rind in medium bowl. Cover, refrigerate 3 hours.

**2** Serve berry mixture with yogurt.

prep time 10 minutes
(+ refrigeration)

nutritional information per serving
101 calories; 24.3g carbohydrate; 3.3g fiber; 0.9g fat (0.3g saturated fat); 2mg cholesterol; 22mg sodium; 2.8g protein; low GI

*tip* Any cranberry juice variation would be suitable for this recipe.

# citrus salad

serves 4

1 medium ruby red grapefruit
(15 ounces), segmented
2 medium navel oranges
(17 ounces), segmented
1 lime, segmented
2 ounces (about ½ cup)
strawberries, quartered
½ cup unsweetened apple juice
¾ cup (6 ounces) low-fat fruit-
flavored yogurt

**1** Combine fruit and juice in
medium bowl. Serve fruit
topped with yogurt.

prep time 15 minutes
nutritional information per serving
112 calories; 25.6g carbohydrate;
3.3g fiber; 0.8g fat (0.4g saturated
fat); 3mg cholesterol; 31mg
sodium; 3.2g protein; low GI

tip If you can't find ruby red
grapefruit (also known as
pink grapefruit), use regular
grapefruit. Any combination
of citrus fruit is fine; mix and
match to suit your taste.

# baked custard

serves 6

6 large eggs
1 teaspoon vanilla extract
⅓ cup superfine sugar
4 cups 1% low-fat milk, heated
¼ teaspoon ground nutmeg

**1** Preheat oven to 325°F. Grease shallow 6-cup ovenproof dish.
**2** Whisk eggs, extract, and sugar in large bowl; gradually whisk in hot milk. Pour custard mixture into dish; sprinkle nutmeg over the top.

**3** Place ovenproof dish in larger baking dish; add enough boiling water to baking dish to come halfway up side of ovenproof dish. Bake about 45 minutes or until custard is set.

prep + cook time 55 minutes
nutritional information per serving
173 calories; 15.7g carbohydrate; 0g fiber; 6.5g fat (2.6g saturated fat); 196mg cholesterol; 158mg sodium; 12.3g protein; low GI

# mango, berry, and passionfruit frozen yogurt

1 small mango (10 ounces)

8 ounces (about 2 cups) strawberries

2 cups (17 ounces) low-fat vanilla-flavored yogurt

¼ cup passionfruit pulp

**1** Blend or process half the mango and half the strawberries, separately, until smooth; finely chop remaining mango and berries. Refrigerate berry puree and berries until needed.

**2** Combine mango puree, chopped mango, and ½ cup of the yogurt in medium bowl; divide mango mixture among eight 1-cup disposable paper cups. Cover, freeze about 1 hour or until surface is firm.

**3** Combine strawberry puree, chopped strawberries, and ½ cup of the yogurt in same cleaned bowl; divide strawberry mixture among the cups. Cover, freeze 1 hour or until surface is firm.

**4** Combine passionfruit pulp and remaining yogurt in same cleaned bowl; divide passionfruit mixture among the cups. Cover, freeze 1 hour. Press popsicle sticks firmly into the mixture in each cup. Cover, freeze 3 hours or overnight.

**5** Remove from cups and serve immediately.

prep + cook time 35 minutes (+ freezing)

nutritional information per cup
86 calories; 16.9g carbohydrate; 1.9g fiber; 1.0g fat (0.5g saturated fat); 3mg cholesterol; 43mg sodium; 3.6g protein; low GI

tip If making individual servings, you need to use eight 1-cup disposable cups, otherwise you can use an 8-inch square cake pan. If using a cake pan instead of the cups, follow the method above, but spread layers into the parchment-paper-lined cake pan. Once frozen, slice and serve immediately.

# vanilla ice cream with mango and berry coulis

serves 6

3 cups 1% low-fat milk
8 ounces soft tofu
¼ cup superfine sugar
1-ounce package sugar-free, fat-free vanilla instant pudding mix
2 teaspoons vanilla extract

BERRY COULIS
10 ounces (about 2 cups) mixed berries
2 teaspoons confectioners' sugar

MANGO COULIS
1 medium mango (15 ounces), peeled, pitted, and coarsely chopped
2 tablespoons water

**1** Put 1 cup of milk, the tofu, and sugar into a blender and blend until very smooth.
**2** Put the pudding mix and remaining milk into a large bowl and whisk constantly for 2 minutes, until set. Whisk in the tofu mixture and vanilla until well combined.
**3** Transfer mixture to 5½-inch x 8½-inch loaf pan. Cover tightly with foil, freeze 3 hours or overnight.
**4** Beat ice cream in large bowl with electric mixer until smooth. Return to loaf pan, cover; freeze an additional 3 hours or until firm. Repeat beating and freezing twice

more. Alternatively, churn ice cream in an ice cream machine according to the manufacturer's instructions.
**5** Make berry and mango coulis.
**6** Serve ice cream with mango and berry coulis.

BERRY COULIS Blend or process berries and sugar until smooth. Push mixture through a fine sieve over small bowl; discard solids.

MANGO COULIS Blend or process mango and the water until smooth.

prep + cook time 40 minutes (+ cooling & freezing)
nutritional information per serving 180 calories; 30.9g carbohydrate; 2.3g fiber; 3.1g fat (0.8g saturated fat); 8mg cholesterol; 266mg sodium; 8.2g protein; low GI

tips Fresh or frozen berries are suitable; if frozen berries are used, they must be thawed before making coulis.

Ice cream and coulis can be made 3 days ahead.

# rosewater and raspberry gelatin    serves 4

6½ ounces (about 1½-cups)
    fresh raspberries
1 cup cranberry juice
2 tablespoons superfine sugar
¼ cup water
3 teaspoons powdered gelatin
2 teaspoons rosewater
2 tablespoons half-and-half

**1** Blend or process 1 cup of the raspberries until smooth. Stir cranberry juice, sugar, and raspberry puree in medium saucepan over medium heat until sugar dissolves. Pour mixture into cheesecloth-lined sieve; stand until mixture has strained through cheesecloth. Discard solids.
**2** Place the water in small heatproof bowl; sprinkle the gelatin over it. Stand bowl in small saucepan of simmering water, stirring, until gelatin dissolves. Stir rosewater and gelatin mixture into strained raspberry mixture.
**3** Divide raspberry mixture among four ½-cup glasses. Cover, refrigerate overnight.
**4** Serve topped with remaining raspberries; drizzle with cream.

prep + cook time 25 minutes
(+ standing & refrigeration)
nutritional information per serving
81 calories; 17.9g carbohydrate;
0g fiber; 0.9g fat (0.5g saturated
fat); 3mg cholesterol; 13mg
sodium; 3.9g protein; low GI

*tip* For a clear gelatin, don't push the mixture through the cheesecloth-lined strainer, instead, allow the mixture to strain gradually; this will take some time.

# baked apples with berries

serves 4

10 ounces frozen mixed berries
4 large apples (1⅓ pounds)
4 cardamom pods
½ cup (4 ounces) plain, low-fat
   yogurt
2 teaspoons honey

**1** Place berries in fine sieve set over small bowl, cover; thaw in refrigerator overnight.
**2** Preheat oven to 325°F.
**3** Core unpeeled apples about three-quarters of the way down from stem end, making hole 1½ inches in diameter. Use small sharp knife to score around center of each apple. Make small deep cut in base of each apple; insert one cardamom pod into each cut.

**4** Pack three-quarters of the berries firmly into apples; place apples in small baking dish. Bake, uncovered, about 45 minutes or until apples are just tender.
**5** Meanwhile, mash remaining berries with a fork in small bowl; stir in yogurt and honey.
**6** Serve apples with yogurt mixture.

prep + cook time  55 minutes (+ refrigeration)
nutritional information per serving
121 calories; 29.8g carbohydrate; 3.7g fiber; 0.9g fat (0.3g saturated fat); 2mg cholesterol; 22mg sodium; 2.5g protein; low GI

# honey buttermilk ice cream with fruit salsa

serves 12

¼ cup water
2 teaspoons powdered gelatin
1½ cups 2% fat evaporated milk
½ cup honey
1½ cups 1% low-fat buttermilk

FRUIT SALSA
1 small pineapple (1¾ pounds),
  coarsely chopped
1 large mango (1⅓ pounds),
  coarsely chopped
3 medium kiwifruit (7 ounces),
  coarsely chopped
8 ounces (about 2 cups)
  strawberries, coarsely chopped

**1** Place the water in small heatproof bowl; sprinkle the gelatin over it. Stand bowl in small saucepan of simmering water, stirring, until gelatin dissolves.
**2** Meanwhile, place evaporated milk in medium saucepan; bring to a boil. Remove from heat; stir in honey and gelatin mixture. Transfer to medium bowl; cool to room temperature.

**3** Beat buttermilk in small bowl with electric mixer until frothy; transfer to large bowl. Beat evaporated milk mixture in large bowl with electric mixer until light and frothy. Gradually beat in buttermilk until combined.
**4** Pour mixture into 8-cup metal container. Cover tightly with foil, freeze 3 hours or overnight.
**5** Beat ice cream in large bowl with electric mixer until smooth. Return to container, cover; freeze an additional 3 hours or until firm. Alternatively, churn ice cream in an ice cream machine according to manufacturer's instructions.
**6** Meanwhile, make fruit salsa. Serve ice cream with salsa.

FRUIT SALSA Combine ingredients in large bowl.

prep + cook time 50 minutes
(+ cooling & freezing)
nutritional information per serving
143 calories; 31.0g carbohydrate; 2.1g fiber; 1.2g fat (0.2g saturated fat); 7mg cholesterol; 71mg sodium; 4.8g protein; low GI

# tiramisu

1 tablespoon instant coffee
powder

¾ cup boiling water

2 tablespoons marsala

9 soft ladyfinger cookies, halved
crosswise

1 cup (9 ounces) low-fat ricotta
cheese

½ cup (4 ounces) light sour cream

2 tablespoons superfine sugar

2 teaspoons cocoa powder

**1** Combine coffee and the water in
medium bowl; stir in marsala.

**2** Stand three ladyfinger halves
upright in each of six ¾-cup
glasses; drizzle the coffee mixture
over the ladyfingers.

**3** Beat cheese, sour cream, and
sugar in small bowl with electric
mixer about 4 minutes or until
mixture thickens slightly.

**4** Divide ricotta mixture among
glasses. Cover, refrigerate 3 hours
or overnight. Serve dusted with
sifted cocoa.

prep + cook time 30 minutes
(+ refrigeration)

nutritional information per serving
149 calories; 20.5g carbohydrate;
0.1g fiber; 4.6g fat (2.7g saturated
fat); 37mg cholesterol; 145mg
sodium; 7.2g protein; medium GI

tips Tiramisu, translated roughly
as "pick-me-up," is usually made
from savoiardi (ladyfinger cookies)
soaked in coffee and marsala,
then layered with masses of
mascarpone and topped with
cream. Our version is no less
delicious . . . but far, far less laden
with fat.

Stir ½ cup pureed fresh
strawberries or mango into the
ricotta mixture.

# glossary

**ALLSPICE** also called pimento or Jamaican pepper; tastes like a combination of clove nutmeg, cumin, and cinnamon – all spices. Available whole or ground.

**BANANA LEAVES** used to line steamers and wrap food; sold in bundles in Asian food shops, greengrocers and supermarkets. Cut leaves, on both sides of center stem, into required sized pieces then immerse in hot water or hold over a flame until pliable enough to wrap or fold over food; secure with kitchen string, toothpicks, or skewers.

**BARLEY** a nutritious grain used in soups and stews (often as a thickener) as well as in whisky- and beer-making. Hulled barley is the least processed form of barley and nutritious and high in fiber. Pearl barley has had the husk discarded and has been hulled and polished, much the same as rice.

**BASIL**
**sweet** the most common type of basil; used extensively in Italian dishes and one of the main ingredients in pesto.
**Thai** also known as horapa; different from holy basil and sweet basil in both look and taste, with smaller leaves and purplish stems. It has a slight aniseed taste and is one of the identifying flavors of Thai food.

**BOK CHOY** also known as buk choy, pak choi, Chinese white cabbage, or Chinese chard; has a fresh, mild mustard taste. Use stems and leaves, stir-fried or braised. Baby bok choy, also known as pak kat farang or Shanghai bok choy, is much smaller and more tender. Its mildly acrid, distinctively appealing taste has made it one of the most commonly used Asian greens.

**BUCKWHEAT** a herb in the same plant family as rhubarb; not a grain so it is gluten-free. Available as flour; ground (cracked) into coarse, medium, or fine granules (kasha) and used similarly to polenta; or groats, which is the whole kernel sold roasted as a cereal product.

**BULGUR** hulled steamed wheat kernels that, once dried, are crushed into various sized grains. Used in Middle Eastern dishes such as kibbeh and tabbouleh. Is not the same as cracked wheat.

**BUTTERMILK** despite its name, buttermilk is actually low in fat, varying between 0.6 percent and 2 percent. Originally the term given to the slightly sour liquid left after butter was churned from cream, today it is intentionally made from no-fat or low-fat milk to which specific bacterial cultures have been added during the manufacturing process.

**CAPERS** the gray-green buds of a warm climate (usually Mediterranean) shrub, sold either dried and salted or pickled in a vinegar brine; tiny young ones, called baby capers, are also available. Rinse well before using.

**CARAWAY SEEDS** small, half-moon-shaped dried seed from a member of the parsley family; adds a sharp anise flavor when used in both sweet and savory dishes.

**CHEESE**
**cheddar** semi-hard, yellow to off-white, sharp-tasting cheese named after the village in Somerset, England, in which it was originally produced. For our lower-fat versions we used one with no more than 20 percent fat.

**cottage** fresh, white, unripened curd cheese with a grainy consistency and a fat content of 15 to 55 percent.
**cream** a soft tart cows'-milk cheese, its fat content ranges from 14 to 33 percent.
**goat** made from goats' milk; has an earthy, strong taste. Available in soft, crumbly, and firm textures, in various shapes and sizes, and sometimes rolled in ash or herbs.
**mozzarella** soft, spun-curd cheese; originating in southern Italy where it was traditionally made from water buffalo milk. Now, generally made from cows' milk, mozzarella is the most popular pizza cheese because of its elasticity and low melting point when heated.
**parmesan** also called parmigiano; a hard, grainy cows'-milk cheese originating in the Parma region of Italy. The curd for this cheese is salted in brine for a month, then aged for up to 2 years in humid conditions. Reggiano is the best parmesan, aged for a minimum 2 years and made only in the Italian region of Emilia-Romagna.
**ricotta** a soft, sweet, moist, cow's milk cheese with a low fat content (8.5 percent) and a slightly grainy texture. The name roughly translates as "cooked again" and refers to ricotta's manufacture from whey that is by-product of other cheese making.

**CHERVIL** also known as cicily; mildly fennel-flavored member of the parsley family with curly dark-green leaves. Available both fresh and dried but, like all herbs, is best used fresh.

**CHICKPEAS** also called garbanzos, hummus, or channa; an irregularly round, sandy-colored legume used extensively in Mediterranean, Indian, and Hispanic cooking. Firm texture even after cooking, a floury mouth-feel and robust nutty flavor; available canned or dried (soak for several hours in water before cooking).

## COCONUT
**cream** obtained commercially from the first pressing of the coconut flesh alone, without the addition of water; the second pressing (less rich) is sold as coconut milk. Available at most supermarkets.
**milk** not the liquid found inside the fruit, which is called coconut juice, but the diluted liquid from the second pressing of the white flesh of a coconut (the first pressing produces coconut cream). Available in cans and cartons.

**FENNEL** also called finocchio or anise; a crunchy green vegetable slightly resembling celery that's eaten raw in salads; fried as a side; or used as an ingredient in soups and sauces.

## FLOUR
**all-purpose** unbleached wheat flour is the best for baking: the gluten content ensures a strong dough, which produces a light result.
**buckwheat** ground kernels of a herb in the same plant family as rhubarb; not a grain so it is gluten-free.
**self-rising** all-purpose plain or whole wheat flour with baking powder and salt added; make it yourself with flour sifted with baking powder in the proportion of 1 cup flour to 2 teaspoons baking powder.
**whole wheat** milled with the wheat germ so it is higher in fiber and more nutritious than plain flour.

**GELATIN** we use dried (powdered) gelatin in this book; it's also available in sheet form known as leaf gelatin. Three teaspoons of dried gelatin (8g or one packet) is about the same as four gelatin leaves. The two types are interchangeable but leaf gelatin gives a much clearer result than dried gelatin; it's perfect in dishes where appearance matters.

**HORSERADISH** a vegetable with edible green leaves but mainly grown for its long, pungent white root. Occasionally found fresh in specialty greengrocers and some Asian food shops, but commonly purchased in bottles at the supermarket in two forms: prepared horseradish and horseradish cream.

**LADYFINGERS** also known as savoiardi, or savoy biscuits, they are Italian-style finger cookies available both crisp and soft.

**LEMON GRASS** also known as takrai, serai, or serah. A tall, clumping, lemon-smelling and tasting, sharp-edged aromatic tropical grass; the white lower part of the stem is used, finely chopped, in much of the cooking of Southeast Asia. Can be found fresh, dried, powdered, and frozen, in supermarkets, greengrocers, and Asian food shops.

**LENTILS** (red, brown, yellow) dried pulses identified by and named after their color.

**LETTUCE**
**iceberg** a heavy, crisp, firm round lettuce with tightly packed leaves.
**mesclun** pronounced mess-kluhn; also known as mixed greens or spring salad mix. A commercial blend of assorted young lettuce and other green leaves, including baby spinach leaves, mizuna, and curly endive.
**romaine** also known as cos lettuce; the traditional caesar salad lettuce. Long, with leaves ranging from dark green on the outside to almost white near the core; the leaves have a stiff center rib giving a slight cupping effect to the leaf on either side.

**MARSALA** a fortified Italian wine produced in the region surrounding the Sicilian city of Marsala; recognizable by its intense amber color and complex aroma. Often used in cooking.

**MIRIN** a Japanese champagne-colored cooking wine, made of glutinous rice and alcohol. It is used expressly for cooking and should not be confused with sake.

**MUSHROOMS**
**button** small, cultivated white mushrooms with a mild flavor. When a recipe in this book calls for an unspecified type of mushroom, use button.
**portobello** large, flat mushrooms with a rich earthy flavor, ideal for filling and barbecuing.
**shiitake** are also known as Chinese black, forest, or golden oak mushrooms. Although cultivated, they have the earthiness and taste of wild mushrooms. Large and meaty, they can be used as a substitute for meat in some Asian vegetarian dishes.

**NOODLES**
**bean thread** also known as wun sen, made from extruded mung bean paste; also known as cellophane or glass noodles because they are transparent

when cooked. White in color (not off-white like rice vermicelli), very delicate and fine; available dried in various size bundles. Must be soaked to soften before use; using them deep-fried requires no pre-soaking.

**soba** thin, pale-brown noodle originally from Japan; made from buckwheat and varying proportions of wheat flour. Comes as dried and fresh, and flavored (for instance, green tea) varieties.

**NORI** a type of dried seaweed used in Japanese cooking as a flavoring, garnish or for sushi. Sold in thin sheets, plain or toasted (yaki-nori).

**POLENTA** also known as cornmeal; a flour-like cereal made of dried corn. Also the dish made from it.

**PRESERVED LEMON** whole or quartered salted lemons preserved in a mixture of olive oil and lemon juice and occasionally spices such as cinnamon, clove, and coriander. Use the rind only and rinse well under cold water before using.

**PROSCIUTTO** a kind of unsmoked Italian ham; salted, air-cured, and aged, it is usually eaten uncooked.

**RICE**
**arborio** small, round grain rice well-suited to absorb a large amount of liquid; the high level of starch makes it especially suitable for risottos, giving the dish its classic creaminess.
**basmati** a white, fragrant long-grained rice; the grains fluff up beautifully when cooked. It should be washed several times before cooking.
**long-grain** elongated grains that remain separate when cooked; the most popular steaming rice in Asia.

**short-grain** fat, almost round grain with a high starch content; tends to clump together when cooked.
**white** hulled and polished rice, can be short- or long-grained.

**RICE PAPER ROUNDS** also known as banh trang, made from rice paste and stamped into rounds; store well at room temperature. They're quite brittle and will break if dropped; dipped momentarily in water they become pliable wrappers for fried food and uncooked vegetables. They make good spring-roll wrappers.

**RISONI** small rice-shaped pasta; very similar to another small pasta, orzo.

**ROLLED BARLEY** flattened barley grain rolled into flakes; looks similar to rolled oats.

**ROLLED OATS** flattened oat grain rolled into flakes and traditionally used for porridge. Instant oats are also available, but use traditional oats for baking.

**ROSEWATER** extract made from crushed rose petals, called gulab in India; used for its aromatic quality in many desserts.

**SAKE** Japan's favorite wine, made from fermented rice, is used for marinating, cooking, and as part of dipping sauces. If sake is unavailable, dry sherry, vermouth, or brandy can be substituted.

**SAUCES**
**fish** called naam pla on the label if from Thailand and nuoc naam if Vietnamese; the two are almost identical. Made from pulverized salted fermented fish; has a pungent smell and strong taste so use according to your taste.

**hoisin** a thick, sweet, and spicy Chinese paste made from salted fermented soy beans, onions, and garlic; used as a marinade or baste, or to accent stir-fries and barbecued or roasted foods.

**soy** also known as sieu, is made from fermented soy beans. Several variations are available in most supermarkets and Asian food stores.

*Japanese soy* an all-purpose low-sodium soy made with more wheat content than its Chinese counterparts; fermented in barrels and aged. Possibly the best table soy to choose if you only want one variety.

*kecap manis* a dark, thick, sweet soy sauce used in most Southeast Asian cuisines. Depending on the manufacturer, the sauces' sweetness is derived from the addition of either molasses or palm sugar when brewed.

*light soy* is fairly thin in consistency and, while paler than the others, is the saltiest tasting; used in dishes in which the natural color of the ingredients is to be maintained. Not to be confused with salt-reduced or low-sodium soy sauces.

*tamari* a thick, dark soy sauce made mainly from soy beans without the wheat used in standard soy sauce.

**sweet chili** sweet comparatively mild, fairly sticky and runny bottled sauce made from red chilies, sugar, garlic, and white vinegar.

**teriyaki** a homemade or commercially bottled sauce usually made from soy sauce, mirin, sugar, ginger, and other spices; it imparts a distinctive glaze when brushed on grilled meat.

**SESAME OIL** made from roasted, crushed, white sesame seeds; used as a flavoring rather than a medium for cooking.

**SWEET POTATO** orange-fleshed potato; good baked, boiled, mashed, or fried similarly to other potatoes.

**TOFU** also known as soybean curd or bean curd; an off-white, custard-like product made from the "milk" of crushed soy beans. Comes fresh as soft or firm, and processed as fried or pressed dried sheets. Fresh tofu can be refrigerated in water (changed daily) for up to 4 days.

**firm** made by compressing bean curd to remove most of the water. Good used in stir-fries as it can be tossed without disintegrating. Can also be preserved in rice wine or brine.

**silken** not a type of tofu but reference to the manufacturing process of straining soybean liquid through silk; this denotes best quality.

**soft** delicate texture; does not hold its shape when overhandled. Can be used as a dairy substitute in ice cream.

## TOMATOES

**bottled pasta sauce** a prepared tomato-based sauce sometimes called ragu or sugo on the label; comes in varying degrees of thickness and flavors.

**canned** whole peeled tomatoes in natural juices; available crushed, chopped, or diced, sometimes unsalted or reduced salt. Use undrained.

**cherry** also known as tiny tim or tom thumb tomatoes; small and round.

**paste** triple-concentrated tomato puree used to flavor soups, stews, sauces, and casseroles.

**plum** also called roma, these are smallish, oval-shaped tomatoes often used in Italian cooking or salads.

**teardrop** small pear-shaped tomatoes.

**TORTILLA** thin, round unleavened bread originating in Mexico; can be made at home or purchased frozen, fresh, or vacuum-packed. Two kinds are available, one made from wheat flour and the other from corn.

**TZATZIKI** Greek yogurt and cucumber dish sometimes containing mint and/or garlic.

**VANILLA**
**bean** dried, long, thin pod from a tropical golden orchid; the tiny black seeds inside the bean are used to impart a luscious vanilla flavor in baking and desserts.

**extract** vanilla beans that have been submerged in alcohol. Vanilla flavoring is not a suitable substitute.

**YOGURT** we use plain full-cream yogurt in our recipes unless specifically noted otherwise. If a recipe in this book calls for low-fat yogurt, we use one with a fat content of less than 0.2 percent.

**ZUCCHINI** the most widely grown type of squash, available year-round in supermarkets.

# index

**HEARST BOOKS**
New York

An Imprint of Sterling Publishing
387 Park Avenue South
New York, NY 10016

Delish is a registered trademark of Hearst Communications, Inc.

www.delish.com

DELISH
Elizabeth Shepard    Executive Director

This book was previously published under the title: *The Australian Women's Weekly The Diabetes Cookbook*

Photography by Stuart Scott
U.S. Edition packaged by LightSpeed Publishing, Inc.; design by X-Height Studio;
Culinary Americanization: Wes Martin
Nutritional Consultant: Joyce M. Vergili, EdD, RD, CDE

10  9  8  7  6  5  4  3  2  1

For information about custom editions, special sales, premium and corporate purchases, please contact Sterling Special Sales Department at 800-805-5489 or specialsales@ sterlingpublishing.com.

Distributed in Canada by Sterling Publishing
c/o Canadian Manda Group, 165 Dufferin Street
Toronto, Ontario, Canada M6K 3H6

Manufactured in China

Sterling ISBN 978-1-61837-073-0

# conversion chart

## Measures

All cup and spoon measurements are level. The most accurate way to measure dry ingredients is to weigh them. When measuring liquids, use a clear glass or plastic measuring cup with markings on the side.

Measurements for cake pans are approximate only. Using same-shaped cake pans of a similar size should not affect the outcome of your baking. We measure the inside top of the cake pan to determine sizes.

We use large eggs averaging 2 ounces each.

## Dry Measures

| IMPERIAL | METRIC |
| --- | --- |
| ½oz | 15g |
| 1oz | 30g |
| 2oz | 60g |
| 3oz | 90g |
| 4oz (¼lb) | 125g |
| 5oz | 155g |
| 6oz | 185g |
| 7oz | 220g |
| 8oz (½lb) | 250g |
| 9oz | 280g |
| 10oz | 315g |
| 11oz | 345g |
| 12oz (¾lb) | 375g |
| 13oz | 410g |
| 14oz | 440g |
| 15oz | 470g |
| 16oz (1lb) | 500g |
| 24oz (1½lb) | 750g |
| 32oz (2lb) | 1kg |

## Liquid Measures

| IMPERIAL | METRIC |
| --- | --- |
| 1 fluid oz | 30ml |
| 2 fluid oz | 60ml |
| 3 fluid oz | 100ml |
| 4 fluid oz | 125ml |
| 5 fluid oz (¼ pint/1 gill) | 150ml |
| 6 fluid oz | 190ml |
| 8 fluid oz | 250ml |
| 10 fluid oz (½ pint) | 300ml |
| 16 fluid oz | 500ml |
| 20 fluid oz (1 pint) | 600ml |
| 1¾ pints | 1000ml (1 liter) |

## Length Measures

| IMPERIAL | METRIC |
| --- | --- |
| ⅛in | 3mm |
| ¼in | 6mm |
| ½in | 1cm |
| ¾in | 2cm |
| 1in | 2.5cm |
| 2in | 5cm |
| 2½in | 6cm |
| 3in | 8cm |
| 4in | 10cm |
| 5in | 13cm |
| 6in | 15cm |
| 7in | 18cm |
| 8in | 20cm |
| 9in | 23cm |
| 10in | 25cm |
| 11in | 28cm |
| 12in (1ft) | 30cm |

## Oven Temperatures

These oven temperatures are only a guide for conventional ovens.
For convection ovens, check the manufacturer's manual.

| | °F (FAHRENHEIT) | °C (CELSIUS) |
| --- | --- | --- |
| Very slow | 250 | 120 |
| Slow | 275–300 | 150 |
| Moderately slow | 325 | 160 |
| Moderate | 350–375 | 180 |
| Moderately hot | 400 | 200 |
| Hot | 425–450 | 220 |
| Very hot | 475 | 240 |